International Labour and Employment Compliance Handbook

www.kluwerlawonline.com

Labour and Employment Compliance in Saudi Arabia

International Bar Association

Labour and Employment Compliance in Saudi Arabia

Second Edition

Sara Khoja
Sarit Thomas

This publication is part of the International Labour and Employment Compliance Handbook, available on www.kluwerlawonline.com

Editors: Salvador del Rey and Robert J. Mignin

International Bar Association
the global voice of the legal profession

Wolters Kluwer

Published by:
Kluwer Law International B.V.
PO Box 316
2400 AH Alphen aan den Rijn
The Netherlands
E-mail: international-sales@wolterskluwer.com
Website: lrus.wolterskluwer.com

Sold and distributed in North, Central and South America by:
Wolters Kluwer Legal & Regulatory U.S.
7201 McKinney Circle
Frederick, MD 21704
United States of America
Email: customer.service@wolterskluwer.com

Sold and distributed in all other countries by:
Air Business Subscriptions
Rockwood House
Haywards Heath
West Sussex
RH16 3DH
United Kingdom
Email: international-customerservice@wolterskluwer.com

Printed on acid-free paper.

ISBN 978-94-035-1581-6

e-Book: ISBN 978-94-035-1582-3
web-PDF: ISBN 978-94-035-1583-0

Printed in the United Kingdom.

All listed titles are also available on lrus.wolterskluwer.com

1. Argentina: Julio César Stefanoni Zani & Enrique Alfredo Betemps, *Labour and Employment Compliance in Argentina, 7th edition*, 2019 (ISBN 978-94-035-1504-5)
2. Australia: John Tuck, Stephen Price, Rosemary Roach, Jack de Flamingh, Nicholas Ellery & Nick Le Mare, *Labour and Employment Compliance in Australia, 4th edition*, 2019 (ISBN 978-94-035-1511-3)
3. Belgium: Chris Van Olmen, *Labour and Employment Compliance in Belgium, 4th edition*, 2019 (ISBN 978-94-035-1514-4)
4. Brazil: Rodrigo Seizo Takano, Andrea Giamondo Massei Rossi & Murilo Caldeira Germiniani, *Labour and Employment Compliance in Brazil, 6th edition*, 2019 (ISBN 978-94-035-1521-2)
5. Canada: Kevin Coon & Adrian Ishak, *Labour and Employment Compliance in Canada, 2nd edition*, 2014 (ISBN 978-90-411-5637-2)
6. Chile: Gerardo Otero A., Maria Dolores Echeverria F., Macarena López M. & María de los Ángeles Fernández S., *Labour and Employment Compliance in Chile, 7th edition*, 2019 (ISBN978-94-035-1524-3)
7. China: King & Wood Mallesons, *Labour and Employment Compliance in China, 5th edition*, 2018 (ISBN 978-94-035-0400-1)
8. England: Tony Hyams-Parish, *Labour and Employment Compliance in England, 7th edition*, 2019 (ISBN 978-94-035-1531-1)
9. France: Pascale Lagesse, *Labour and Employment Compliance in France, 7th edition*, 2019 (ISBN 978-94-035-1534-2)
10. Germany: Gerlind Wisskirchen & Martin Lützeler, *Labour and Employment Compliance in Germany, 7th edition*, 2019 (ISBN 978-94-035-1541-0)
11. India: Manishi Pathak, *Labour and Employment Compliance in India, 7th edition*, 2019 (ISBN 978-94-035-1544-1)
12. Ireland: Duncan Inverarity & Sinéad Grace, *Labour and Employment Compliance in Ireland, 6th edition*, 2019 (ISBN 978-94-035-1551-9)
13. Israel: Yaron Horovitz, Pnina Broder-Manor & Helen Raziel, *Labour and Employment Compliance in Israel, 6th edition*, 2019 (ISBN 978-94-035-1554-0)
14. Italy: Angelo Zambelli, *Labour and Employment Compliance in Italy, 7th edition*, 2019 (ISBN 978-94-035-1561-8)
15. Japan: Yoshikazu Sugino, *Labour and Employment Compliance in Japan, 7th edition*, 2019 (ISBN 978-94-035-1564-9)
16. Republic of Korea: Sang Wook Cho, Soojung Lee & Christopher Mandel, *Labour and Employment Compliance in the Republic of Korea, 5th edition*, 2019 (ISBN 978-94-035-1601-1)
17. Mexico: Oscar De La Vega Gómez, *Labour and Employment Compliance in Mexico, 7th edition*, 2019 (ISBN 978-94-035-1571-7)
18. The Netherlands: Els de Wind & Cara Pronk, *Labour and Employment Compliance in the Netherlands, 4th edition*, 2018 (ISBN 978-94-035-0470-4)
19. Poland: Barbara Jóźwik, *Labour and Employment Compliance in Poland, 7th edition*, 2019 (ISBN 978-94-035-1574-8)

20. Russia: Anna-Stefaniya Chepik, *Labour and Employment Compliance in Russia*, 2013 (ISBN 978-90-411-4925-1)
21. Saudi Arabia: Sara Khoja & Sarit Thomas, *Labour and Employment Compliance in Saudi Arabia, 2nd edition,* 2019 (ISBN 978-94-035-1581-6)
22. South Africa: Susan Stelzner, Stuart Harrison, Brian Patterson & Zahida Ebrahim, *Labour and Employment Compliance in South Africa, 7th edition*, 2019 (ISBN 978-94-035-1584-7)
23. Spain: Salvador del Rey, Ana Campos & Sergi Gálvez Duran, *Labour and Employment Compliance in Spain, 7th edition*, 2019 (978-94-035-1591-5)
24. Turkey: Sertaç Kökenek & Elif Nur Çakır Vurgun, *Labour and Employment Compliance in Turkey, 5th edition*, 2019 (ISBN 978-94-035-1614-1)
25. United Arab Emirates: Sara Khoja & Sarit Thomas, *Labour and Employment Compliance in the United Arab Emirates, 6th edition*, 2019 (ISBN 978-94-035-1604-2)
26. United States: Baker & McKenzie LLP, *Labour and Employment Compliance in the United States, 4th edition*, 2018 (ISBN 978-94-035-0483-4)

International Bar Association
The Global Voice of the Legal Profession

The International Bar Association (IBA), established in 1947, is the world's leading organization of international legal practitioners, bar associations and law societies. The IBA influences the development of international law reform and shapes the future of the legal profession throughout the world. It has a membership of over 40,000 individual lawyers and almost 200 bar associations and law societies spanning all continents. It has considerable expertise in providing assistance to the global legal community.

Grouped into two divisions – the Legal Practice Division and the Public and Professional Interest Division – the IBA covers all practice areas and professional interests, providing members with access to leading experts and up-to-date information. Through the various committees of the divisions, the IBA enables an interchange of information and views among its members as to laws, practices and professional responsibilities relating to the practice of business law around the globe. Additionally, the IBA's high-quality publications and world-class conferences provide unrivalled professional development and network-building opportunities for international legal practitioners and professional associates.

The IBA's Bar Issues Commission provides an invaluable forum for IBA member organisations to discuss all matters relating to law at an international level.

The IBA's Human Rights Institute (IBAHRI) works across the Association, to promote, protect and enforce human rights under a just rule of law, and to preserve the independence of the judiciary and the legal profession worldwide.

Other institutions established by the IBA include the Southern Africa Litigation Centre and the International Legal Assistance Consortium.

Employment and Industrial Relations Law Committee

The aims of the committee are to develop and exchange knowledge of employment and industrial relations law and practice. Members support each other through the provision of innovative ideas and practical assistance on day-to-day issues. In addition, through its journal and through presentations, conferences, the committee ensures the dissemination of up-to-date law and practice in this highly important business area.

International Bar Association Global Employment Institute

The IBA Global Employment Institute (IBA GEI) was formed in early 2010 for the purpose of developing for multinationals and worldwide institutions a global and strategic approach to the key legal issues in the human resources and human capital fields.

Drawing on the resources and expertise of the IBA membership, the IBA GEI will provide a unique contribution in the field of employment, discrimination and immigration law, on a diverse range of global issues, to private and public organizations throughout the world. The IBA GEI is designed to enhance the management, performance and productivity of these organizations and help achieve best practice in their human capital and management functions from a strategic perspective.

The IBA GEI will become the leading voice and authority on global HR issues by virtue of having a number of the world's leading labour and employment practitioners in its ranks, and the support and resource of the world's largest association of international lawyers.

Further information

International Bar Association, 4th Floor, 10 St Bride Street, London EC4A 4AD, United Kingdom, Tel: +44 (0)20 7842 0090, Fax: +44 (0)20 7842 0091, E-mail: member@int-bar.org, www.ibanet.org

About the International Labour and Employment Compliance Handbook

From 1976 through 1988, the International Bar Association and Kluwer Law International published the groundbreaking International Handbook on Contracts of Employment. This Handbook provided one of the first global overviews of the law of the international employment relationship.

Since publishing the first edition, globalization of business has created an increased demand for knowledge of labor and employment laws throughout the world. Therefore, along with Kluwer, we decided to publish an updated Handbook which we have titled the International Labour and Employment Compliance Handbook.

This new Handbook was intended to be a practical guide by providing a general overview of key labor and employment issues in multiple jurisdictions. Each chapter was written so that it is easy to understand by lawyers and non-lawyers alike. Each country author has also followed a standard outline to assist readers in analysing employment issues in each country.

The first edition of this new Handbook included nineteen (19) different countries.

This Handbook would not have been possible without the help and assistance of many people. Most importantly, the individual country authors are all distinguished legal practitioners who spent considerable time drafting and revising their country reports to meet difficult deadlines. We thank each of them. Our friends at Kluwer, especially Ewa Szkatula, have done a wonderful job in keeping the editors and the authors on schedule. Finally, we want to also express our gratitude to Cuatrecasas, Gonçalves Pereira, and Baker & McKenzie LLP for their valuable assistance in the coordination and organization of this project. Our warmest thanks to each of them.

Because of the success of the Handbook, Wolters Kluwer Law & Business decided to publish each country report also as a separate book to give a choice in obtaining the information. We hope this new format will be a helpful and useful resource just like the Handbook. Both formats are available in print and online.

The Editors

Salvador del Rey Guanter
Robert J. Mignin

March 2013

Saudi Arabia

AUTHORS

Sara Khoja

Sara Khoja specializes in employment law, advising corporate clients in a variety of sectors, including oil and gas, construction, hospitality, retail, technology, shipping and insurance. She qualified in England and Wales in 2002.

She is a partner in the employment practice for Clyde and Co LLP's Middle Eastern and African Offices in the United Arab Emirates, the State of Qatar, the Kingdom of Saudi Arabia and the Sultanate of Oman. Clyde and Co LLP is the largest international law firm in the Arabian Gulf region and has had a presence in the region for over thirty years. Sara is based in Clyde and Co's Dubai office, having joined in 2008 when the practice was established, where she provides employment advice for the Middle East region, and in particular the Arabian Gulf Cooperation Council Member States. Sara provides advice on all aspects of employment law, including recruitment, termination, terms and conditions of employment (benefits, bonuses and remuneration), and the application of quotas for the employment of nationals in various Arabian Gulf countries.

Sara also has a particular focus on multi-jurisdictional projects and issues arising out of employee mobilization, including the territorial reach of UK employment law.

She regularly presents at seminars and workshops as part of Clyde and Co's regular client programme; and at external events organized by various business councils and HR consultancy firms. She has written for a number of publications, including the *New Law Journal*, *Asian Counsel*, *Solicitors Journal* and *Personnel Today*. She is also regularly quoted in publications such as *Gulf News*, *Gulf Business*, and *Emirates 24/7*.

ADDRESS

Sara Khoja,
Partner,
Employment Group,
Clyde & Co LLP,
Dubai Office: PO Box 7001, Level 15, Rolex Tower, Sheikh Zayed Road, Dubai, United Arab Emirates,

Tel.: + 971 50 552 9961
Fax: +971 4 384 4004
E-mail: Sara.Khoja@clydeco.ae

Sarit Thomas

Sarit is a Professional Support Lawyer within the Clyde & Co LLP knowledge management team based in the firm's Dubai office, within the employment department. Sarit is admitted to practise as a solicitor in England and Wales and has been based in the Middle East region since 2008.

Sarit's role includes the creation of precedent documentation, researching and advising on recent developments in employment law and keeping the employment team's knowledge and skills up-to-date. As part of her role, Sarit organizes, prepares and delivers training both internally to the firm and externally at client seminars, as well as managing the team's internal training programme. Sarit also prepares and delivers training programmes with the Dubai Legal Affairs Department to registered lawyers in Dubai. Sarit writes legal articles and contributes to the team's client bulletins, as well as to a number of external legal publications, and is responsible for keeping the team's knowledge and skills up-to-date and managing the team's know-how and template database.

ADDRESS

Sarit Thomas,
Professional Support Lawyer,
Clyde & Co LLP,
Dubai Office: PO Box 7001, Level 15, Rolex Tower, Sheikh Zayed Road, Dubai, United Arab Emirates,

Tel.: + 971 56 548 8158
Fax: +971 4 384 4004
E-mail: sarit.thomas@clydeco.com

Table of Contents

Legal Compliance in the Kingdom of Saudi Arabia

1. LEGAL FRAMEWORK: EMPLOYMENT LAWS IN KSA

The Kingdom of Saudi Arabia (KSA) is the largest Arab state by land area, constituting the bulk of the Arabian Peninsula. KSA has an estimated population of 30 million, of which approximately one-third are foreign nationals. In late April 2015, Saudi Arabia's Deputy Crown Prince Mohammed bin Salman announced an ambitious and groundbreaking programme to develop the Kingdom's economy and society over the coming years ('Vision 2030'). Vision 2030 seeks to reduce the overall unemployment rate from 11.6% to 7%, overhaul the education system and increase the female participation rate from 22% of the workforce to 30% and to create more employment opportunities for Saudi Arabian youth in general.

The KSA legal system is a Sharia'a law system following the Hanbali school of law, with the Koran providing the most important source of law. Royal and Ministerial Decrees are periodically issued to meet the complexities of modern life and commercialized business transactions. Such Decrees are only valid if they do not conflict with Sharia'a law.

The employment relationship is governed primarily by Royal Decree No. M/5123 Sha'ban 1426 / 27 September 2005, as amended (the 'Labour Law'), which covers all aspects of employment and the employment relationship, including employment contracts, wages and benefits, leaves, working hours and the termination of employment. The Labour Law became effective as of September 2005, replacing the previous labour law of 1969, and it is administered and enforced by the KSA Ministry of Labour and Social Development (MOLSD). A series of significant amendments were introduced in April 2015, and they became effective in October 2015 (the

'2015 Amendments'). Ministerial Resolution Number 88478 dated 1/5/1439 (equivalent to 9 February 2015) was also issued supplementing existing fines under the Labour Law and immigration regulations.

In addition, Ministerial Resolution No. 88478 of 1/5/1439 H, approving the new violations and penalties schedule of the Labour Law is also in force, and new implementing regulations to the Labour Law ('Implementing Regulations') were issued pursuant to Ministerial Resolution No. 70273 dated 11/04/1440 H (corresponding to 18 December 2018) which was published on 11 January 2019, replacing the previous implementing regulations (Ministerial Resolution No. 1982, as amended). The Implementing Regulations are in force from the date of their publication, being 11 January 2019.

The Labour Law applies to all employers and employees in the KSA, except expatriates who enter the KSA to perform specific tasks limited to a duration of two months (for example, those on business visas or temporary work visas) and domestic servants (for example, maids and drivers).

The Labour Law and the Implementing Regulations set out an employee's minimum entitlements, and employers are free to confer different terms on an employee as long as they are more generous to the employee.

There are no free zones or secondary jurisdictions which affect or alter the application of the Labour Law in KSA. However, a number of new economic cities have been announced, most notably the King Abdullah Economic City, in order to encourage foreign direct investment, but these are not free zones as such, and the laws of KSA apply equally within these new localities.

2. CONTRACTS OF EMPLOYMENT

2.1. Overview

As defined by the Labour Law, employment relationships in Saudi Arabia are created by a 'contract concluded between an employer and an employee, whereby the latter undertakes to work under the management or supervision of the former for a wage'. Furthermore, 'the employment contract shall be in duplicate, with one copy to be retained by each of the two parties. However, a contract shall be deemed to exist even if not written. In this case, the employee may establish the contract and his entitlements arising therefrom by all methods of proof. Either party may at any time demand that the contract be in writing.' As such, whilst employment contracts may be written or oral, and an employee may provide any evidence in support of an oral contract, including testimony as to oral agreements entered into, in order to prove the existence of the contract, without a written employment contract, it is practically extremely difficult for an employee to establish his or her status and also his or her entitlements. It is, therefore, preferable to have in place a written employment contract.

Arabic is the official language for the contract, employment data, records and other documents. Foreign language versions may be provided for the benefit of the employees; however, in the event of a labour dispute or conflict between the two versions, the Arabic text prevails.

2.2. Written Employment Contracts

Employment contracts should be executed in duplicate, one copy to be retained by each of the parties to the contract. The 2015 Amendments state that the MOLSD will develop a standard uniform employment contract. This model contract was published as part of the Implementing Regulations and identifies clauses which are optional or compulsory. The model contract is not a prescribed form contract, nor must it be registered. However, it must be shown to the MOLSD as part of the recruitment process and employee registration process by the employer with the MOLSD and the social security authority; General Organisation for Social Insurance (GOSI).

Employment contracts for non-KSA nationals must be fixed-term contracts. If an employment contract does not specify the term, the duration is equal to that of the employee's residency visa and work permit.

Contracts for KSA nationals can be unlimited or for a fixed period (whether that be for a specified duration or for a specified task). Contracts for specific tasks terminate upon completion of the task. If a fixed-term contract is renewed for three consecutive terms or if the employee enters into a fixed-term contract which will take his continuous employment service to four years, the employee is automatically regarded as a permanent employee.

A contract with a non-KSA national cannot be converted into an unlimited term contract as it will always be deemed limited to the term of the work permit and residency visa.

MOLSD Contract

The contract is five pages long with eight main clauses which are identified as being either compulsory, optional or to be chosen depending on whether the contract is a fixed term or an unlimited term.

The eight clauses are:

(1) contract purpose and subject which sets out the role, whether the contract is fixed term or unlimited together with the start date of employment and the probationary period;

(2) days and hours of work on a daily or weekly basis. This clause also confirms the entitlement to overtime payable at the rate of a 50% surplus on the basic pay (more detail in section 10.3);
(3) duties of the employer which include paying the stated remuneration (which can also be expressed on a piecemeal basis); awarding annual leave, private medical insurance, registering the employee with GOSI, covering all recruitment costs, visa costs, repatriation costs (including if the employee dies), awarding maternity leave (and breastfeeding leave) if applicable, and awarding bereavement leave;
(4) duties of the employee which include performing work to the best of his ability and in line with instructions, taking care to preserve all equipment and property of the employer, working to the best of his ability to avoid any threat to health and safety, to undergo medical examinations at the employer's request both before the employment starts or during the employment designed to ensure that the employee is fit to perform his job, to adhere to local customs and abide by laws and work regulations of the employer, agreeing to the employer deducting as necessary GOSI contributions through payroll;
(5) termination of contract whether on expiry of the fixed term or by written notice. This clause sets out the employer's right to terminate under Article 80 of the Labour Law and the entitlement of the employee to terminate under Article 81 of the Labour Law. Importantly, this clause also provides for the employer and employee to agree on the compensation payable for unjustified termination of the employment;
(6) end of service gratuity;
(7) the application of the Labour Law, the model work regulations and the Implementing Regulations in conjunction with the provisions of the contract; and
(8) process or format for communications between the employer and employee, importantly the employee is under a duty to inform the employer of his current or updated contact details.

2.3. Oral Contracts

Oral contracts are binding. However, employment contracts for non-KSA nationals should be in writing and subject to a specified term. KSA employees may establish the contract and its entitlement arising under it by all methods of proof and either party may at any time demand that the contract be in writing.

2.4. Employee Handbooks

Pursuant to the 2015 Amendments, employers are required to have in place company bylaws in compliance with the prescribed model work regulations prepared by the MOLSD. The model work regulations have fifty-six regulations and an attached table of applicable disciplinary fines. An employer may adopt the model work regulations or prepare its own version, provided they comply with the provisions of the Labour Law and Implementing Regulations, and provided such regulations are reviewed and attested by a MOLSD approved law firm and thereafter by the MOLSD. Any regulations issued by an employer which are contrary to the Labour Law or the Implementing Regulations are void. The employer is also obliged to communicate such bylaws or any amendments thereto to its employees, by displaying the same in a prominent location.

The model work regulations are extensive, and some of its notable provisions include the following:

(1) clarification that a repatriation ticket is not payable by the employer if an employee resigns without reason during the probationary period, or if the employee is not capable of performing the role he was recruited into, or if his repatriation is due to his violation of a law and a fine being imposed whether administrative or criminal;
(2) eligibility criteria for promotion and the selection of equal candidates for promotion;
(3) employee performance assessment system and yearly appraisals;
(4) clarification that nursing breaks following a return from maternity leave are applicable whether the employee's baby is being breastfed or bottle fed and, that it is the employee's duty to provide written notice to the employer requesting the break and when she would like to take it during the working day;
(5) a duty on all employees to follow and adhere to Islamic principles and morals of behaviour and, a duty for men and women not to be alone together in the workplace; and
(6) a duty on employers to inform employees and instruct them on what is acceptable behaviour in the workplace and in particular about instructing employees on the prohibition on any form of harassment or action which would undermine dignity and morals or any form of assault or harm of another employee.

2.5. Job Descriptions

Job descriptions are not mandatory. However, such documents are commonly issued in the KSA, depending on the employer's custom and practice. Certain functions may only be undertaken by Saudi nationals. These roles are primarily limited to administrative functions such as human resources and finance management, but also include, for example, security guards. There are currently approximately eighteen roles reserved for Saudi nationals. The MOLSD in January 2017 published job descriptions for each of these roles and stated in its guidance that it would examine the substance of what a person does rather than the label or title given, making it harder for employers to employ non-KSA nationals in reserved roles. The reserved roles are (1) Senior Executive Human Resources, (2) Employee Affairs Manager, (3) Labor Affairs Director, (4) Personnel Relations Manager, (5) Personnel Affairs Specialist, (6) Personnel Affairs Clerk, (7) Employment Clerk, (8) Employees' Affairs Clerk, (9) Attendance Clerk, (10) General Reception Clerk, (11) Hotel Reception Clerk, (12) Patients Reception Clerk, (13) Complaints Clerk, (14) Treasurer, (15) Private Security Guard, (16) Commentator, (17) Key Maker, and (18) Customs Broker.

2.6. Offer Letters

It is not mandatory to issue offer letters in the KSA, although it is commonplace for employers to do so.

2.7. Checklist of Do's and Don'ts

(1) Ensure that all written offer letters and employment contracts are clear and consistent.
(2) Ensure that all documents issued to an employee are consistent with the terms of the MOLSD Contract and the prescribed model work regulations described above in section 2.4.

3. RECRUITING, INTERVIEWING, SCREENING AND HIRING EMPLOYEES

3.1. Overview

Immigration in the KSA is sponsorship based, known as 'Khafala'. A local Saudi entity or individual is required to sponsor short-term and long-term employment engagements, short-term engagements being those where business visas, commercial visit visas and work visit visas are satisfactory.

The MOLSD has introduced an online system whereby all visa and permit applications are now undertaken via an online portal. This system has improved the process significantly; it has made the process more transparent as well as improving communication between the various government departments. The new system has also increased focus on Saudization and ensuring employers are compliant with their Saudization requirements and targets.

a. General Requirements

The local KSA entity must have a registered Government Relations Officer (GRO) to act as the principal liaison between the entity and local authorities where necessary.

Employers sponsoring individuals for long-term work are required to ensure that the local entity has executed an employment contract with the individual employee, the sponsor must provide the employee with local health insurance, social security enrolment, and (in most instances, depending on the company size) local payroll through the country's Wage Protection System (WPS).

Sponsored individuals may only work for, and at the premises of, the sponsoring entity. Secondment of employees (i.e. work has to be undertaken on client site) is permitted in certain circumstances. A process known as 'Ajeer' must be followed which is the technical process whereby an individual sponsored by Company A can work at Company B's site.

Immigration / labour checks may be carried out at random or planned (generally as a result of non-compliance reports).

KSA does not have visas on arrival or visa exemptions. All foreign nationals are required to obtain a visa in advance of entry into the country. Golf Corporation Council (GCC) nationals (save for Qatari nationals) are the exception as they may travel freely into KSA without the need for a visa; however, they are still required to comply with certain procedures in order to obtain approval to work.

b. Work Permit and Iqama

Long-term work engagements in the KSA require the procurement of a work permit and Iqama (residence permit). Work permits and Iqamas are in principle valid for a period of one year and are renewable upon expiry. The MOLSD has introduced a residence card which is issued to the employee. This residence card has a validity period of five years; however whilst the card is valid for five years, the work permit still requires renewing every year (but no new card will be issued until it expires unless the employee changes employer).

All work permits result in the establishment of a formal 'employment' arrangement with the local sponsoring entity to which local law applies.

In order to employ foreign nationals, host sponsoring entities must first obtain authorization to do so by applying for a block visa.

c. Block Visas

This document provides the authorization for the employment of foreign nationals. Block Visa is where approval for multiple applicants is granted in one document for specific roles within a company. The Block Visa is granted on the basis of very specific criteria, namely job role, gender and number of positions as per the list of job titles issued by the Ministry of Labour. Previously, the nationality was also required on initial application, but this detail can now be specified in the second stage once the block is granted, and it is allocated to specific individuals.

Stage one involves the electronic filing of the block visas requests together with the relevant supporting documents. The company at this stage is required to state the number of positions required, job titles and gender. It is worth noting that the MOLSD may not always approve the same number of positions applied for (e.g. if ten visas are applied for, six may be granted). Once these positions are approved stage two requires the company to allocate such positions to specific nationalities and obtain approval from the MOLSD and the Ministry of Interior (MOI – nationalities could be rejected at this stage as the government monitors the makeup of nationalities carefully within an employing entity and also within the country as a whole). Upon allocation, the block visa is valid for two years, but in some instances where for example the block visa is issued for specific projects (for example, government-related projects), the visa may be valid for the duration of the specific contract. In order to be eligible for a block visa companies are generally required to demonstrate compliance with the following:

(1) only companies classified as medium green and above within the Saudization programme (further detail below) may apply for block visas. The hiring of non-Saudi nationals must not impact the employer's categorization such that it would fall below the medium green category;

(2) the professions being applied for should neither be amongst those for which there are Saudi nationals qualified and willing to perform the role; nor be amongst those professions which are restricted to Saudi nationals only;

(3) the company should have a valid business reason to request the block visa quota- there must be a business need to employ a number of foreign nationals;
(4) the company should be in compliance with taxation (Zakat), social security, Saudization, have a valid Commercial Registration and evidence this through appropriate certificates obtained from the respective government departments;
(5) the sponsoring entity should have adequate office space to accommodate the total number of employees. There is no particular ratio which Ministry of Labour looks at; however, when providing the documents, the Ministry of Labour will want to see the floor plan.

Obtaining block visas may be a relatively time-consuming process. The approval takes on average between one and four weeks depending on the block visa type, the entity's eligibility and rating (public holidays may affect this timeframe).

Previously there was only one type of block visa, whereas now there are different categories. All applications are generally filed electronically. The various types of block visas are as follows:

Establishment block visa

These are granted to newly established entities in order to facilitate the recruitment of foreign nationals. To be eligible for this type of block visa, the entity must have:

(1) employed at least one Saudi national;
(2) no record of employing foreign nationals previously; and
(3) apply within six months of incorporation.

Expansion or Private Sector contracts block visa

This is the most common type of block visa application which is granted to entities wishing to sponsor more foreign national employees due to the expansion of their business, either by way of extension of a current project or securing a new one.

A sponsoring entity must show a valid business need justifying its request to sponsor additional foreign nationals. In practice, this is evidenced by showing a business contract with another private entity in the KSA (not with a non-KSA entity).

Government Project block visa

This visa is granted to entities where such entity has either (i) contracted with a government entity or (ii) contracted as a subcontractor with an entity which has contracted directly with a government entity.

Government Support block visa

Certain entities may fall under the ambit of a particular government body due to its commercial activity or operational structure; for example, engineering companies must register with the Saudi Council of Engineers (SEC). Such companies may apply for this type of block visa via their applicable government body.

d. Work Permit Overview

Once the block visa is approved, reflecting the job titles and gender, the host entity may then proceed with the allocation of the positions to the designated foreign nationals. Following the issuance of the block visa, the foreign national must secure a work (entry) visa enabling him to enter the KSA and complete the in-country formalities pending issuance of the final work permit and Iqama.

The process for obtaining a work visa, work permit, and Iqama is quite time consuming and document intensive. Both the sponsoring employer and the foreign national employee must meet the conditions of eligibility, being:

(1) employees must hold job-related degree certificates as detailed on the block visa;
(2) employees must be within the permitted age range (generally between 22 and 60);
(3) employees must be medically fit and not have a contagious medical condition; and
(4) employees must not have a criminal record; a police clearance from the country of origin is required.

In some instances, further conditions may be imposed.

Application procedure

Before a non-KSA national arrives in KSA, the sponsor must apply for an entry work visa with the relevant KSA consular post abroad. Various documentation will need to be submitted which may vary from consular to consular. In most instances, the employee is required to undergo a medical test (including a blood test for infectious diseases such as HIV) and produce a medical report in a prescribed form from the employee's country of origin and also obtain a police clearance report from the country of origin. In addition, certain job titles will require the presentation of appropriate academic credentials that have been legalized by the KSA consular post in the country of issuance.

Upon review of the application and supporting documents, a single entry work visa is issued by the KSA embassy in the individual's country of origin and endorsed on the applicant's passport, at which time the applicant has ninety days to enter the country and apply for the work permit and Iqama, which must be obtained within three months of entry. Upon entry into KSA, the individual must supply their fingerprint details and also undergo an eye cornea scan and registration.

In order to apply for the work permit and Iqama, the employee must complete the in-country formalities which can be undertaken online on the Ministry of Labour, MOI and Muqeem websites. In most instances, the employee will need to undertake another medical examination (the results of which are uploaded online) and be registered, by the sponsor, with an authorized health insurance provider (all employees and dependants must have health insurance). The sponsor must file an electronic request for the work permit with the Ministry of Labour. On issuance an electronic request for the Iqama must then be filed with the MOI and the physical residence card is then sent by post (if the sponsor is situated in Riyadh) or the sponsor can collect the same directly from the immigration department.

The employee cannot exit the country until such formalities have been completed. In a straight forward case, in-country processing takes about seven to ten working days to complete. Employees cannot work until they have received their Iqama and sponsored individuals may only work for, and at the premises of, the sponsoring entity. Secondment of employees is permitted in certain circumstances.

e. Short-Term Visas

In addition to the work visa described above, short-term visas are also available. Those wishing to visit KSA for a short term may opt to obtain a visit visa. Visit visas, in the context of corporate immigration, may either be for commercial purposes or for work visits. Visas on arrival are not permitted, and similarly, KSA does not have a tourist visa category (aside from religious tourism or very limited commercial tourism). However, GCC nationals do not require a visa in order to enter the country and reside, but they are required to complete certain formalities in order to work in the country.

The following short-term visas are available.

Commercial Visit Visa

This visa does not permit the individual to work, but the individual may carry out business activities. The regulations do not provide an exhaustive list of the types of activities that may be conducted whilst on this visa, but activities such as conducting face to face meetings, attending seminars and conferences, conducting research and site visits are generally considered permissible in practice. This type of visa is issued at the discretion of the consulate and usually allows for multiple entries into the country. The duration of this type of visas differs according to the nationality of the applicant.

Work Visit Visa

This visa permits temporary hands-on work for short-term projects at the site of the sponsoring entity.

The validity period for both the Commercial Visit Visa and the Work Visit Visas will vary and the authorized period of in-country stay will generally be between thirty and ninety days from date of entry.

f. Dependants and Family

An employee can apply for a dependent residence permit or for short-term family visas once in the country, and once the Iqama has been issued.

g. Sponsorship Transfer within Saudi

Local hire is common in Saudi Arabia, but the consent of the existing employer is required in order for the employee to transfer his visa to a new employer. However, employers will frequently refuse to effect a transfer in order to cut an employee out of the market. In such an instance, the individual has to leave the KSA and have the new employer process a fresh application for him to return to the Kingdom. The advantage of sponsorship transfer is that a block visa is not required, and the new employer does not have to use an existing visa quota to recruit someone from the country. However, the company must still be compliant with its Saudization targets. Companies with a low green rating or lower (*see* section 3.2 below for definitions) are not permitted to take advantage of this facility. Employees working for an entity with a low Saudization rating (i.e. red) may leave and transfer to a higher rated company without the requirement of having to obtain permission from the old employer.

Certain employers in the Kingdom are now also eligible to replace a departing employee with a new one without having to obtain a separate block visa approval. The process referred to as 'a replacement block visa' was recently reinstated, after the MOLSD suspended it in 2015. Only companies in specific industries, including engineering, medicine and pharmaceuticals, information and technology, medical technology, accounting and financing, classified under a low green or higher rating, can benefit from this scheme.

h. Immigration Restrictions

Foreign nationals must procure a multiple exit/re-entry permit in order to facilitate travel to and from the KSA which must be obtained and granted by the employer. A foreign national cannot leave the country without first obtaining an exit permit. In instances where an employee's Iqama is being cancelled, the employee's dependants will need to ensure that they leave with or prior to the employee and in any event prior to the cancellation of the employee's Iqama. Dependants cannot stay in the country following the employee's exit (i.e. to complete the school term).

Breach of the regulations relating to immigration and the employment of foreign nationals is taken very seriously in KSA and can have significant consequences for both the employer and its employees.

Any company or sponsor that employs a foreign national, who does not have an up-to-date (i.e. current) residence permit or visa or work permit, will be punished with a fine of SAR 20,000 for each illegal employee. In addition, the Ministry of Labour reserves the right to levy any further punishment on the employer that it deems appropriate in the circumstances. Any employer engaging a foreign individual without work and residency authorization of any nature is subject to higher fines (SAR 100,000) and employers violating immigration rules can be banned from Government contracts for five years.

All individuals concerned, normally the prospective employee, those responsible for the recruitment of the employee and those with the power of authorization, risk 'stern punishment' and criminal prosecution likely to result in deportation back to their home country and a period of imprisonment pending deportation (if they are not KSA nationals).

3.2. Recruitment

An employer is under a duty to consider KSA nationals for all vacancies prior to engaging a foreign national. Until recently, all vacancies were required to be posted with the Human Resources Development Fund (HRDF) (through their Taqat recruitment portal) and advertised for a period between seven and forty-five days (depending on the employing entity's category) to unemployed KSA nationals registered with the HRDF before a non-KSA national could be offered the role. However, this requirement of conducting labour market testing and advertising has recently been suspended, allowing companies operating within the private sector to reduce the timelines for processing new work permits and Iqamas.

The non-Saudi employee can be employed and undertake work only as stipulated in the work permit.

a. Employment of KSA Nationals

The main HR challenge in the KSA is a shortage of both skilled and specialized labour, due in large part to the lack of relevant curricula at state educational institutions and the average Saudi's historic reluctance to enter technical vocations. A rapidly growing population (over 50% of which is under age 25), and declining oil revenue (per capita) is making it difficult to maintain the prevailing standard of living, and high levels of unemployment and underemployment, particularly amongst young workers are exacerbating economic and social tensions.

In response, the KSA government created its Saudization policy in 1996 to encourage employers in the private sector to hire KSA nationals over non-KSA nationals. As stated above, an employer is under a duty to consider KSA nationals for all vacancies prior to engaging a foreign national. The Saudization policy initially required any employer with twenty or more employees to meet specified hiring quotas which started at 5% of the workforce and required that the percentage of Saudi national employees be increased by 5% per year. The Labour Law introduced in 2005 subsequently specified that the percentage of KSA workers should be 75%. However, the Labour Law also provides that in cases where adequately qualified workers are not available, or it is otherwise not possible to fill vacant jobs, the Minister of Labour may reduce this percentage.

The 75% Saudization requirement has proved to be impossible to uniformly implement in practice. For a period temporary exemptions reduced this requirement to 30% of the total workforce and in some sectors (such as foodstuffs, beverages, textiles and garment manufacture) reduced the requirement to 20%, but such exemptions have now expired. Instead, it is now typical for such Saudization requirements to be determined on a periodic basis, initially upon the licensing of new business and subsequently upon the issuance of a Saudization certificate. The MOLSD typically approaches the issue on a sector by sector basis (and also considers the size of the workforce) and under the Nitaqat system, which loosely translates to 'points' (implemented from August 2011 pursuant to Ministerial Resolution No. (4040), as amended) it will place employers within a category according to how it assesses the particular employer's compliance with its obligations to employ KSA nationals. The categories range from platinum, green (high, medium and low), yellow and red. Generally, an employer benefits from being in a higher category by enjoying greater flexibility in relation to recruiting and managing expatriate employees and will face increasing sanctions when placed in a lower category.

Until 2 February 2019, the Saudization policy provided for Saudization to be calculated based on a twenty-six-week rolling average. The number this generated then determined the employer's Nitaqat rating, and as a result, recruiting and removing Saudi nationals did not instantly change the employer's rating, as the process was gradual and only reflected after twenty-six weeks (or six months). This delayed any new Saudi national recruits from counting towards the employer's workforce immediately, as the employer had to wait for twenty-six weeks from the date the Saudi national is registered with GOSI **for the effect on their Nitaqat rating to be seen. However, the MOLSD announced that as of 2 February 2019 the effect of any new recruits and/or departures would reflect immediately on the company's Nitaqat rating.**

b. Quotas for KSA Nationals and Reservation of Roles in the Private Sector

There are certain roles in KSA that are reserved for KSA nationals (approximately 18 – *see* section 2.5). The employment of KSA nationals in the private sector is increasingly regulated and monitored. The MOLSD are strict with regard to reserving certain roles for KSA nationals and are therefore highly unlikely to issue a work permit to a non-national for any such a role.

In general:

(1) Every employer will be required to have at least one Saudi national employee regardless of the size of the employer, and this employee must be engaged in order to open an employer file with the MOLSD.
(2) Certain functions may only be undertaken by KSA nationals. These roles are primarily limited to administrative functions such as human resources and finance management, but also include, for example, security guards and secretaries.
(3) An employer is under a duty to employ a KSA national before employing a non-KSA national for a job.

(4) All vacancies must now be posted with the HRDF (*see* section 3.2 above).

c. Nitaqat System

Quotas under Nitaqat are set according to an employer's commercial activities and also its size. The MOLSD made changes to the Nitaqat system in September 2017 by increasing the mandatory employment ration of Saudi nationals to expatriate employees. Nitaqat classifications now apply to employers with six employees or more and, quotas have been significantly increased. In many sectors, a quota which previously saw an employer fall into a high green or even platinum category has been downgraded to a low green category following these changes unless the employer increases its Saudi national headcount. Only employers classified as high green or platinum may apply for block visas. The company size thresholds can be summarized as follows:

(1) very small-sized category 1A (5 employees or less);
(2) small-sized category 1B (6–49 employees);
(3) medium-sized category 2A (50–99 employees);
(4) medium-sized category 3B (100–199 employees);
(5) medium-sized category 4C (200–499 employees);
(6) big-sized category 5 (500–2999 employees); and
(7) huge-sized category 6 (3000 or more employees).

Failure to achieve target results in the employer being unable to renew sponsorship of existing employees or to obtain sponsorship for new employees.

Employers who are part of a corporate group with more than one entity or branch can be categorized into existing entities and combined existing entities. The key point is that on a combined basis within a corporate group or where the entities are linked to the same owner and establishment or reference number, the Saudization quota will be applied to establishments within the group with the same sector activities and on the basis of headcount. For example, within a corporate group, one branch and one subsidiary may retain sector activities, and these will be looked at on a combined basis so that the Saudization target would be higher than if the two establishments were looked at separately.

In assessing an employer's achievement of quota (which is essentially based on a points system), the following factors are taken into account:

(1) In order to be counted towards Saudization, the Saudi national employee must be registered with GOSI and be paid a minimum basic salary of SAR 3,000 a month for working on a full-time basis. A

part-time Saudi employee paid SAR 1,500 is counted as half an employee or half a point.

(2) The number of foreign employees is referenced to the employees registered with the National Information Centre at the MOI.

(3) An employer cannot remain without at least one Saudi employee on its records.

Special Categories under Nitaqat

A part-time employee may not be taken into account when calculating the Saudization rate in more than two entities.

Student employees are taken into account as half a point provided they are paid SAR 1,500. They can only count towards one entity's Saudization rate. Student employees can account for up to 10% of the total Saudi workforce under these provisions. For students over 10%, they will not count towards an employer's Saudization quota. In nutritional service industries, students can make up to 40% of the Saudi workforce.

Disabled Saudi employees will count as four Saudi employees provided they are registered with GOSI as disabled and have a GOSI certificate to this effect. Once the number of disabled employees reaches 10% of the Saudi workforce, the individual disabled employee will only count as one employee. This category of employee can only be counted towards one employer's quota.

Released convicts for a period of two years from the date of such person's release from prison, count as two Saudi employees up to a maximum of 10% of the Saudi workforce. Thereafter the individual would count as one employee in the usual way.

With the three special categories above, the first employee in the category to go over the 10% threshold will still attract the increased points for the employer. All three of these special category employees are also looked at as a group such that their combined numbers cannot reach more than 15% of the total Saudi workforce in any one employer.

The following categories are counted as Saudi nationals (i.e. required to be GOSI registered and paid SAR 3,000 or SAR 1,500 as a full-time or part-time employee): (a) GCC nationals, (b) spouse of Saudi national, and (c) children of Saudi female.

Certain nationalities such as Burmese Muslims and Palestinians are also counted towards quota, counting 0.25 of a point towards achievement of quota.

There is also a specific regulation relating to female and disabled employee remote workers. Under this resolution, female and disabled employees (regardless of gender) will count towards Saudization subject to caps set according to the employer's Nitaqat category. The table below sets out the relevant caps. The key in remote working arrangements is that the employer must be able to prove that the employee is in fact doing substantive work and is not what is often described as a 'shadow' worker.

Nitaqat Category	*Percentage*
Platinum	Percentage of Regulated Remote Workers should not exceed 30% of the total Saudi national employees
Green	Percentage of Regulated Remote Workers should not exceed 20% of the total Saudi national employees
Yellow and Red	Percentage of Regulated Remote Workers should not exceed 10% of the total Saudi national employees

As stated above, depending on its compliance with its Saudization quota, an employer is then placed in a category with the implications of each category set out below.

Category	*Impact*
Red	– Can't change expatriates professions – Can't transfer expatriate services – Can't apply for new visas – Can't apply for work permits – Can't open a file for a new company or branch – Can't renew existing expatriates work permits/visas
Yellow	– Suspended from receiving new visas – Can't transfer expatriate services – Can't change existing expatriate professions – Renew existing expatriates work permits – remaining period on residence is 180 days – Can't renew existing expatriates work permits if they have 2 years in KSA – Can't issue work permits for new expatriates

Category	*Impact*
Low Green	– Block visa not possible – The ability to amend the profession of expatriate employees – A grace period of six months: the Certificate of Zakat and income – Recruit expatriates working for entities in the Yellow or Red categories: no need for no objection certificate (NOC) – Renew work permits (residency should have 180 days) – Employee transfer possible if former employer's consent not required or former employer in the low green range, or lower
Medium Green	– Block visa possible – The ability to amend the profession of expatriate employees – A grace period of six months: the Certificate of Zakat and income – Recruit expatriates working for entities in the Yellow or Red categories: no need to NOC – Renew work permits (residency should have 180 days) – Replacement block visa – sector specific
High Green	– Block visa possible – 1 visa back for every 2 cancelled – The ability to amend the profession of expatriate employees – A grace period of six months: the Certificate of Zakat and income – Recruit expatriates working for entities in the Yellow or Red categories: no need for NOC – Renew work permits (residency should have 180 days) – Replacement block visa – sector specific

Category	*Impact*
Platinum	– New visas for any profession required by the employer – Amend stated professions on visas – Recruit from Red/Yellow category employers; no NOC – 12 months grace period: certificate of Zakat and income tax – Renewing residency periods of expatriates (6 months left) – Replacement block visa – sector specific

d. Parallel Saudization

The MOLSD introduced a new programme called 'Parallel Nationalization' in September/ October 2017 which aims to help employers who are unable to meet the requirements of the Nitaqat programme (namely the achievement of quotas set according to employer size and sector). The programme allows employers to pay fees in order to upgrade their classification within Nitaqat.

These fees will be determined according to how many KSA nationals would need to be employed in order for the employer to move to the higher or next classification category under Nitaqat. The fees are subject to change each month. However, employers have the option of paying such fees six months in advance for the Nitaqat classification to be upgraded accordingly.

The programme is designed to make one unit of Parallel Nationalization equal to one Saudi national under Nitaqat. The calculation method is based on specific criteria in the electronic calculator on the MOLSD's website with one unit being determined by the number of KSA nationals already employed within the particular establishment. By way of example, if an employer has ten KSA nationals, and needs to add three nationals to move to the next Nitaqat category, the first unit will be 10%, the second 20% and the third 30%. The final cost will be the total of all units.

The levies or subscription costs within this new system are high and depending on the number of KSA nationals required to achieve a certain Nitaqat classification, it may well be that it is more economical for an employer to hire more KSA nationals rather than subscribe to this new programme or to aim to maintain a high green Nitaqat category rather than aiming for platinum.

An increasing measure being introduced by the MOLSD is to entirely Saudize certain activities within retail. Such activities currently include the sale and maintenance of mobile phones and their accessories, retail sale of female clothing (by female Saudi employees). From 1/1/1440 H (approximately mid-August 2018) the following retail activities must be performed by Saudi nationals: sale of children and male clothing, sale of motorbikes and cars, sale of household goods and office furniture, sale of household hardware. From 1/3/1440 H retail sale of glasses, watches and electronics must be Saudized. From 1/5/1440 H, retail sale of medical equipment, building materials and construction materials, car parts, confectionary and patisserie or sweet places and carpets.

3.3. Employment Applications

There are no specific legislative provisions regarding processing employment applications or considering them. The duty to employ KSA nationals and recruit them is set out above.

Most employers will adopt a streamlined process applicable across their operations in all jurisdictions, with standard application forms, interview format and questioning.

3.4. Pre-Employment Inquiries

There is no legislation restricting the information an employer may request from an employee. The information gained must be held in accordance with data protection legislation and privacy rules applicable in the country where the recruitment is taking place. Within the Kingdom, there is as yet no comprehensive data protection legislation applicable within the employment context. However, Islamic Sharia law recognizes a right to privacy. It should also be noted that the immigration process for sponsoring an individual to work and reside in the Kingdom will require the submission of extensive personal information including an individual's religion (a religion must be stated in the application) and the submission of a certificate of good conduct showing the person is free of criminal conviction.

3.5. Pre-employment Tests and Examinations

There is no legislation restricting the information an employer may request from an employee. The information gained must be held in accordance with data protection legislation and privacy rules.

3.6. Background, Reference and Credit Checks

The Labour Law does not place any limitation on information an employer can request from an applicant nor does it impose any limitations on employers that wish to check the employment references and information presented by applicants. The following checks may be conducted:

a. Criminal Records

Police clearance certificates are available, but only in limited circumstances. A certificate of good conduct is required as part of the work permit and residency visa application process.

b. Medical History

Under the immigration procedures, non-Saudi national employees must undergo a medical check. When an expatriate is recruited, he or she must obtain a medical examination certificate in his or her home country including a negative test for contagious diseases (particularly HIV) and up-to-date vaccinations (including meningococcal, hepatitis A and B and, depending on the home country, typhoid).

c. Drug Screening

The law does not expressly prohibit drug screening and, given the serious attitude of the Saudi authorities towards drug possession, pre-employment drug testing is unlikely to result in a backlash against the employer. Alcohol is also prohibited in Saudi Arabia. Employers can carry out random drug and alcohol testing of employees using the MOLSD's accredited system and registered government-designated clinics. This service is particularly common in the oil and gas industry.

d. Credit Checks

The Saudi Credit Bureau offers consumer credit information services in Saudi Arabia.

e. Immigration Status

Employers are required to secure work and residence permits for foreign employees brought into the country. A non-Saudi national employee must carry his or her residence permit for identification purposes at all times. –The recently published Implementing Regulations explicitly prohibit the retention of foreign national Employees' passports, Iqama or medical insurance card. The previous implementing regulations, whilst prohibiting such practice, provided a template consent form for employees to sign to agree to their employer holding their passport whilst employed. Such a facility has been removed by the new Implementing Regulations. Employers are keen to hold employees' passports until the employee leaves the country, as employers are liable for the administrative cost of the employee's exit and re-entry.

f. Social Media

With respect to the privacy and monitoring the employee's use of the internet, the main body of law in the KSA is the Islamic Sharıah. Sharıah principles protect individuals' right to privacy and prohibit disclosure of secrets, save where the owner's consent has been obtained or where such disclosure is required due to the public interest.

The Saudi cybercrime legislation imposes criminal penalties on those who invade privacy by using recording equipment or intercepting electronically transmitted data without authorization. The courts may also apply the principles of Sharia law. As a general principle of Sharia law, an employer is liable for any damage directly suffered by an employee as a consequence of the employer's actions.

Employers should include provisions in employment contracts concerning monitoring and privacy in the workplace. On the proviso that any amendments to such policy are approved by the MOLSD, the employer can seek to restrict the use of the internet and social media during working hours by incorporating such restrictions in the internal labour policy and the employee's contract of employment.

g. Interviewing

There is no obligation to interview employees prior to offering them jobs. There is also no specific legislation in this area governing the format of an interview, questions to be avoided or which must be asked. Due to sponsorship processes, it is common to ask candidates if they are married or single, and in some instances their age. In common with other employee processes, many employers will operate a standard process across their multi-jurisdictional operations determined by company needs and business unit structures.

3.7. Hiring Procedures

As referred to above in section 3.1, once an employee is extended an offer of employment, the sponsorship application process must be commenced. Before a non-KSA national arrives, the sponsor must apply for prior approval for their entry from the MOLSD. As part of the application process, the employee is required to undergo a medical test (including a blood test for infectious diseases such as HIV) and submit a medical report in a prescribed form from their home country. The entry visa is therefore issued by the KSA embassy in the individual's country of origin. Once an entry visa has been obtained, the employee may enter and work in KSA, as long as the work permit and Iqama (identity card and residency visa) are applied for and obtained within three months of entry. Upon entry into KSA, the individual must supply their fingerprint details and also undergo an eye cornea scan and registration.

3.8. Fines and Penalties

Breach of the regulations relating to immigration and the employment of foreign nationals is taken very seriously in KSA and can have significant consequences for both the employer and its employees, including fines, imprisonment and deportation.

3.9. Checklist of Do's and Don'ts

(1) Obtain references and criminal record checks for all new employees.
(2) Require employees to submit authenticated and attested professional and educational certificates.
(3) Carry out credit checks for employees engaged in financial or accounting roles.
(4) Hold all information in strict confidence, inform employees of the information collected, and how it will be held.

4. MANAGING PERFORMANCE/CONDUCT

4.1. Overview

As described in section 2.4 above, employers are required to have in place company bylaws in compliance with the prescribed model work regulations prepared by the MOLSD and the Labour Law. The Labour Law sets out various provisions pertaining to the disciplinary process employers are expected to follow and permitted disciplinary actions. The model work regulations are available for employers to adopt, or they can opt to prepare their own subject to approval (as described in section 2.4 above). Broadly the Model Work regulations provide for the following:

a. Appraisal System

Every employee should be assessed formally and in writing at least once a year; with the appraisal covering the following:

(1) the individual's ability to perform work and their level of proficiency;
(2) the employee's conduct, cooperation with colleagues, customers, and managers; and
(3) the individual's punctuality.

Each employee should be given a performance marketing or ranking based on five performance gradings, which are broadly described as being high performance, upper intermediate, intermediate, lower intermediate, and poor.

b. Reward and Promotion

The model work regulations seek to regulate the payment of bonus payments in that the regulations provide that an employee ranked as intermediate should be eligible for a bonus where an employer operates a bonus scheme. The amount and method for calculating any bonus is for the employer to determine and indeed, whether or not to provide any bonus scheme at all is at the employer's discretion.

Internal promotions are also regulated by the model work regulations and linked to the performance management and assessment scheme. Where a role is vacant, then an employee is able to apply for it on the basis that it is a higher ranking role for which he is appropriately qualified and has achieved a performance ranking in his last appraisal of 'upper intermediate' and the promotion is approved by the General Manager. If there are competing internal applications for the same role, the model work regulations provide that the following factors should be taken into account: which employee has achieved a higher appraisal ranking, has higher educational qualifications, experience, seniority within the organization and the authorized (i.e. line of report) manager's view.

c. Employment Termination due to Performance

Where an employee's performance warrants review, it is worth noting that the Labour Law and the model work regulations envisage the employer following the same process as that which applies for disciplinary matters. Whilst poor performance and misconduct are conceptually different, the procedure to document an employer's steps to remedy them are the same under the Labour Law and the model work regulations. A three-step process involving inviting an employee to a meeting in writing and outlining the concerns, meeting with the employee to give him an opportunity to explain the situation and make any representations he may have and finally confirming the employer's decision in writing, should be followed. There are also time limits to take into account such as the requirement that any procedure is initiated within thirty days of the employer becoming aware of the employee's poor performance. The model work regulations contain a table providing guidance on the type of sanction applicable for various acts by an employee and, where poor performance is involved, an employer would be expected to issue written warnings identifying the skill gap and what needs to be done by the employee to address it. An employer would also be expected to provide training and support to an employee in order to improve his performance and where possible, even consider moving him to a role more in line with his capabilities.

Generally, prior to considering termination by reason of poor performance, an employer would be expected (depending on the surrounding circumstances) to have issued at least two written warnings over a six month period. Where a warning or sanction is issued (of whatever nature), these are valid or 'live' for a period of one hundred and eighty days following which they can remain on an employee's file, but they are not 'live' warnings upon which further action can be based.

4.2. Coaching and Counselling

There is no requirement to provide coaching or counselling for a poorly performing employee. Employers' practices in this area differ and larger multinational employers will often apply performance improvement plans providing for mentoring, coaching and counselling.

4.3. Written Evaluations

Appraisals or written evaluations are widely used in order to assess employees' performance. Such documents can be used in order to justify an employee termination for poor performance provided the written documents set out clearly any performance concerns and the actions the employer may take in response if no improvement is made.

4.4. Warnings and Suspensions

Under the Labour Law and the model work regulations, an employer must follow a minimum procedure involving, setting out the performance concerns in writing, meeting with the employee to hear his representations regarding the concerns, and then confirming any decision in writing. Disciplinary sanctions include written warnings, denial of promotions by up to a year, withholding or postponing allowances for a term not exceeding one year, suspension without pay and dismissal.

4.5. Checklist of Do's and Don'ts

(1) Companies should ensure that they have in place company bylaws in compliance with the prescribed model work regulations prepared by the MOLSD.
(2) Assessing performance or addressing poor performance should be undertaken in accordance with the model work regulations and the Labour Law.
(3) Ensure that procedures are documented and warnings are issued in writing.
(4) If termination is a possibility, this should be communicated in writing and clearly expressed.

5. TERMINATION OF EMPLOYEES FOR PERFORMANCE OR DISCIPLINARY REASONS

5.1. Overview

Employers are permitted to terminate a contract of employment only for specified reasons. These are:

(1) If both parties thereto agree to terminate it, provided that the worker's consent is in writing.
(2) If the term specified in the contract expires, unless the contract has been explicitly renewed in accordance with the provisions of the Labour Law in which case it shall remain in force until the expiry of its term.
(3) At the discretion of either party to the indefinite term contracts in pursuance of the provisions of Article 75 of the Labour law.
(4) The worker attains the age of retirement, which is sixty years for males and fifty-five years for females unless the two parties agree upon continuing work after this age. The retirement age may be reduced in cases of early retirement as provided for in the work-organizing bylaws. If it is a fixed-term employment contract, which extends beyond the retirement age, it shall terminate at the end of its term.
(5) Force majeure.
(6) The firm is closed down.
(7) The completion of the business, in which the employee has engaged in unless agreed otherwise.
(8) Any other case to be provided for by any other law.

Employers may terminate employees without notice, compensation in lieu of notice, or end of service gratuity, in the following circumstances:

(1) during the probationary period (each party has the right to terminate employment during the probationary period unless the employment contract reserves the right to only one party);
(2) as a result of assaults on the employer, the employer′ managers, or any superiors;
(3) due to the failure to perform essential work duties or obey orders;
(4) due to misconduct or acts of dishonesty or lacking integrity;
(5) as a result of intentional acts with the intent of causing material loss for the employer;
(6) for forgery in support of obtaining employment;
(7) on the basis of absence from work without valid reason for more than thirty days in a year or fifteen consecutive days, provided the

employee receives written warning prior to termination ten or five days beforehand, respectively;

(8) for disclosure of work-related industrial or commercial secrets; and
(9) for taking unlawful advantage of his employment position for financial gain.

However, employees must be given the opportunity to object to the reasons for termination. It is also important to note that any disciplinary investigation must commence within thirty days of the discovery of the offence and any disciplinary sanction must be issued within thirty days of the conclusion of the investigation. With the exception of termination for just cause, the employment of pregnant female employees may not be terminated during the one hundred and eighty-day period preceding the date of delivery. Equally, employees on sick leave cannot be terminated due to illness until the full entitlement to sick leave has been exhausted.

There are no separate rules for the dismissal of individuals in managerial, executive, or board member roles. Common practice on termination of employment is the same as that for lower level employees where it is common to make a payment on account of statutory entitlements plus a compensatory payment for termination that covers any other entitlements.

5.2. Separation/Severance Pay

Under the Labour Law, end of service gratuity is payable to all employees. The payment is equal to half a month of pay per year for the first five years of service and one month of pay per year of service thereafter (pro-rated for any partial year of service). The gratuity is calculated on the basis of the last wage including regularly paid allowances, such as housing and transportation allowances, and must be paid within one week of the termination of the contract (a longer period applies where the employee resigned).

To the extent that the employee's remuneration includes elements that are variable (such as commission or bonus), it is permitted to provide in the employment contract for such elements to be excluded for the purposes of calculating the end of service gratuity.

If the employee terminates voluntarily i.e. resigns, the benefit is reduced by two-thirds for periods of service of two to five years, and by one-third for periods of service between five and ten years. Employees who resign with ten or more years of service are entitled to the full benefit. All payments due to the resigning employee must be paid within two weeks of the termination of the contract. There are exceptions to these reductions where the employee resigned due to reasons of force majeure (or the effects of this).

Female workers who terminate their contract within six months of marriage or three months of giving birth and all workers that terminate their employment due to a force majeure are also entitled to full benefits.

Employees on fixed-term contracts are eligible for end of service gratuity equal to fifteen days' pay for the first five years of service and thirty days' pay per year of service thereafter (pro-rated for any partial year of service).

5.3. Fines and Penalties

Where an employee considers that they have not been terminated for a 'valid reason', the employee may bring a claim in KSA through the Commission for the Settlement of Labour Disputes (Labour Commission) for unjustified dismissal.

If successful, the employee may be awarded compensation. This compensation is in addition to the end of service gratuity and notice. In the case of an unlimited contract, compensation will be fifteen days' pay for each year of service. Where the contract is for a fixed duration, the compensation could be equivalent to the salary that the employee would have received for the remaining duration of the fixed term. In both cases, the minimum amount that will be awarded will be two months' wages.

Prior to the introduction of the 2015 Amendments, it was relatively rare in practice for awards to be made for the full remaining duration of the fixed-term contract. The 2015 Amendments significantly changed the compensation due on termination for an invalid reason by introducing a set formula under Article 77 of the Labour Law (as amended) for compensation in the event of unjustified termination. Parties may expressly state in the employment contract the level of compensation which may be payable where either party terminates the contract without reason, provided that it must not be less than two months' wages.

5.4. Checklist of Do's and Don'ts

(1) Always document poor performance or misconduct.
(2) Comply with internal disciplinary and performance management procedures and model work regulations.
(3) Consider any potential discriminatory impact of performance assessment measures and any potential for a termination to be unfair or discriminatory.
(4) Set out the reason for dismissal in the termination letter.

(5) Document final payments made to an employee, calculation methods and obtain employee sign off.

6. LAYOFFS, REDUCTIONS IN FORCE AND/OR REDUNDANCIES AS A RESULT OF JOB ELIMINATIONS OR OTHER RESTRUCTURING

6.1. Overview

The 2015 Amendments allow the employer to terminate the employment contract validly if the business is closed permanently or the business unit or operation in which the employee is employed is closed or eliminated (e.g., through outsourcing). This recognition of redundancy does not go as far as to extend to situations where there is a reduction in work requirements that requires a reduction in the workforce or a reduction in a particular role. The KSA courts have recognized an employer's right to reorganize its business and restructure, resulting in the elimination of roles. However, a high burden of proof is applied, and the employer's business decision is scrutinized very closely. In any case, as a matter of best practice and to reduce the risk of successful unjustified dismissal claims, an employer should meet with its employees and follow a consultation process.

However, where an employee is a KSA national, a recent resolution limits the ability of employers in the Kingdom to collectively terminate KSA national employees' employment by reason of redundancy. In any case other than an employer's bankruptcy and the closure of the employing establishment entirely, the resolution prohibits large and medium-sized entities from making collective redundancies of KSA nationals for any reason (other than poor performance or misconduct) connected to the economic condition of the employer, without first informing the local labour office at least sixty days prior to serving written notice of termination and following their process and recommendation. Under the resolution, collective dismissal means, terminating groups of KSA nationals for reasons related to the employer and not to the employees (in other words for restructuring or redundancy purposes). A group will exist if the proposed terminations are of more than 1% of the KSA national employees or a total of ten employees whichever is greater within one year from the date of the last termination of a KSA national.

When notifying the local labour office of the intended dismissals, an employer must include the following documents and information with its notice:

(1) a financial study from the employer explaining the reasons for the proposed collective dismissals;

(2) name and numbers of KSA nationals who will be terminated with the job description and reasons for termination for each one;
(3) name and numbers of none KSA nationals with their job description who are at the same level of the KSA nationals who will be terminated; and
(4) the procedure or steps taken by the employer to avoid the terminations.

Within forty-five days of the notice, the labour office will evaluate the risks and issue an opinion to the employer about its proposal. The opinion will be based on the following:

(1) the financial position of the employer;
(2) the possibility of finding alternative solutions by replacing none KSA nationals with KSA nationals.
(3) the possibility of finding alternative positions for the KSA nationals within the entity, or in another entity owned by the employer; and
(4) the possibility of a settlement with the KSA national employees who will be terminated.

A commission for reviewing employer notices and providing opinions on such notices, will be formed in each labour office around the Kingdom and its members will be as follows:

(1) the manager of the labour office;
(2) representative of the HRDF branch; and
(3) a legal counsel.

The commission has the power to do the following:

(1) Call the employer's representative to discuss the reasons for proposing collective dismissals as well as how the employer can justify terminating KSA national employees.
(2) Propose an alternative, in consultation with the employing entity to avoid the termination.
(3) Review the employer's notice and assign a legal expert to give his opinion; according to the Labour Law and its Implementing Regulations, and in accordance with this resolution and other rules and regulations.
(4) Reject the notice and the reasons for terminating KSA national employees.
(5) Accept the notice and the entity's reason for terminating KSA national employees.
(6) Develop a plan to address the effects of the termination of KSA national employees if the commission is convinced by the reasons presented by the employer for the collective dismissals.

6.2. Reductions in Force/Layoffs/Job Eliminations

In the absence of legislative provisions, reductions in work hours, variations in work patterns and sabbaticals or absence without pay or reduced pay, are all matters for contractual negotiation and agreement with individual employees.

6.3. Fines and Penalties

There is no requirement for reporting business reorganizations or restructuring resulting in redundancies or mass layoffs; nor is there a requirement to inform and consult regarding redundancy proposals; accordingly, no fines or penalties apply for failure to take any of these measures.

When a business makes redundancy terminations, the potential fine or penalty is the exposure to claims of arbitrary termination. Where a KSA national is being terminated, the above-mentioned reporting procedure will have to be considered. The MOLSD may impose penalties for companies that violate this process, including blocking the employer's ability to apply for new work permits or transfer sponsorships to it for a period of between thirty and three hundred and sixty days depending on the seriousness of the violation. If an employer breaches the requirements and effects collective dismissals of 15% to 20% of its Saudi national workforce without prior approval, it will be barred from applying for new work permits, accepting visa transfers or being able to object to its employees transferring sponsorship without its approval for five hundred and forty days. Where an employer collectively dismissed over 20% of its Saudi national workforce without following the new requirements, these penalties will also apply, in addition to a bar on the employer being able to renew existing work permits, for seven hundred and twenty days.

6.4. Checklist of Do's and Don'ts

(1) Always document the termination procedure and reason for dismissal.
(2) Consider adopting a redundancy policy as a matter of company policy.
(3) Follow personnel best practice in adopting a process to explain to employees the redundancy situation and its effect on the business.

(4) When selecting an employee for redundancy out of a group of employees, have a clear and documented process for selecting this employee out of many.
(5) Follow the termination procedure for KSA nationals.

7. LABOUR AND EMPLOYMENT LAW RAMIFICATIONS UPON ACQUISITION OR SALE OF BUSINESS

7.1. Overview

Article 18 of the KSA Labour Law provides for employees to transfer by operation of law from one employer to another, pursuant to a change in the corporate ownership of the employer or the part of the business in which they are employed (including the sale of a business or part of a business as a going concern, and the merger of two companies, or demerger). However, such transfer is only possible upon a special application to the MOLSD whose approval is discretionary, and it can take up to two years for the process to be completed. In the absence of Article 18 applying, transfer of employees is effected through a process of termination and re-hire.

On a general note, due diligence regarding labour and employment matters can often be overlooked in this region when considering whether or not to acquire a business. Such oversights lead to practical difficulties once a business is acquired and potentially the company taking on liabilities it had not envisaged.

7.2. Acquisition of a Business

Acquisition through a share purchase does not affect the employees who continue being employed by the same entity on the same terms and conditions and are simply inherited by the purchaser.

7.3. Acquisition Checklist

(1) A purchaser should always carry out due diligence on the employees it will inherit, the status of such employees and the status of the business with the MOLSD (i.e., its Saudization compliance, whether it has registered violations and fines) and the GOSI.
(2) Accrued liability for end of service gratuity should be investigated and also whether such liability has been recorded in the businesses' accounts and records.

(3) Due diligence should also cover the key terms and conditions of employees (particularly senior management) and identify any unusual terms and conditions of employment, for example, benefits cover, commission arrangements and bonus arrangements. Employees' nationalities should also be requested as well as each employee's visa status.
(4) Due diligence should also identify whether any employees are international assignees, with underlying employment contracts in another jurisdiction or if employees are dual contract employees, having a local KSA contract and also a contract with an offshore holding company or 'mother' company. Such arrangements give potential scope for dual claims.
(5) Due diligence should cover any current or potential disputes with employees and the existence or otherwise of post-termination restrictions in key personnel's contracts.
(6) If the business is being bought in its entirety (through share purchase), a purchaser should ensure that the trade licence of the business covers the activities the employees are carrying out and the actual business being conducted.

7.4. Sale of a Business

As stated above, Article 18 of the Labour Law provides for employees to transfer by operation of law from one employer to another, pursuant to a change in the corporate ownership of the employer or the part of the business in which they are employed (including the sale of a business or part of a business as a going concern, and the merger of two companies, or demerger). There is no approval required from Saudi authorities for the transfer of Saudi nationals.

In terms of consultation, the Labour Law does not lay down any specific time frame or process for consultation or providing notice to employees when it comes to the transfer of their employment.

7.5. Sale Checklist

(1) A seller will need to know whether the purchaser intends to take on any of the employees currently employed within the business being sold and the terms and conditions on offer to employees.
(2) Consider reflecting the liabilities the seller will face (e.g., having to make redundancies post-sale or to pay out accrued employment

entitlements on completion) in the commercial terms and the sale price.

8. USE OF ALTERNATIVE WORKFORCES: INDEPENDENT CONTRACTORS, CONTRACT EMPLOYEES, AND TEMPORARY OR LEASED WORKERS

8.1. Overview

Due to the immigration framework requiring sponsorship for work and residency for any non-KSA national to be provided by a KSA national or a KSA entity, in practice, the use of atypical workers is unusual. Any foreign individual provided with sponsorship for work and residency will de facto be an employee of the sponsor. KSA and GCC nationals whilst they do not require such sponsorship must be registered as employees with MOLSD and GOSI or have commercial licences in their own right to run businesses of their own accord.

There are around sixteen manpower supply companies licenced in the Kingdom, and there is also a system known as ‘Ajeer’ permitting the secondment of employees so that effectively an employee can be sponsored by company A but working at company B. In addition, part-time working is permitted as is freelancing for Saudi nationals.

8.2. Independent Contractors

The key for an individual to be an independent contractor is for the individual to hold his or her own independent commercial registration such that they can carry out business on their own account. Since October 2017, the MOLSD has also introduced a system whereby Saudi nationals can register with it to be freelancers. There are seventy-eight activities which can be carried out by freelancers.

a. Definition

There is no express definition of ‘freelancer’, but the MOLSD has stated in its publications that freelancer work is work that is carried out by individuals which is specialist and technical such that individuals can be engaged to provide advisory or consultancy services. In order to be recognized as a freelancer, the individual has to register electronically with the MOLSD providing his or her Saudi ID details, educational qualifications and applying for a freelancer certificate. Once this is granted, they are then free to contract as freelancers with individuals or corporate entities.

b. Creating the Relationship

Once the individual has a freelancer certificate, he will be recognized as a consultant and can engage to provide their services. Employers should be careful to engage freelancers under written agreements setting out their freelancer status, the services to be delivered and the fee to be paid. The agreement should expressly state that the individual is not an employee and include their freelancer registration details.

c. Compensation

The Labour Law provisions will not apply to freelancers, nor will they be counted towards any Saudization targets. There are, therefore, no regulations regarding their compensation or engagement and the financial consideration is to be determined freely under a written agreement. Freelancers should not be registered by the corporate entities engaging them with GOSI. The freelancer can himself register with GOSI and apply for subsidies or support in paying their GOSI contributions.

d. Other Terms and Conditions

These are free to be determined under the contract. The Labour Law does not regulate the engagement of freelancers, and they would not be entitled to any Labour Law entitlements such as leave (of any kind), end of service gratuity or any other benefits.

8.3. Contract Workers

Part-time employees are regulated by a specific MOLSD resolution which provides that an employer may engage part-time employees who are regarded as employees working lesser hours than a full-time employee (as defined by the employer). In order to be recognized as a part-time employee, the employer and employee must enter into a written agreement expressly designating the individual as part-time, and be for a limited duration. The employee will be entitled to the protection of the Labour Law's provisions on rest breaks, leave entitlements, health and safety and workmen's compensation. However, the other provisions of the Labour Law will not apply.

8.4. Leased Workers

The MOLSD has licensed around sixteen companies to provide manpower supply services. In order to hold such as licence, the entity must be owned entirely by Saudi nationals and have a Saudi national as the General Manager. It must also have a high capitalization and directly sponsor and employ the individuals it supplies to its clients. One key consideration in using a manpower supplier is that it is required to report to the MOLSD on its clients and the resources supplied to them such that it cannot act as a mechanism for entities to circumvent their Saudization obligations. The MOLSD will link the headcount supplied through manpower suppliers with the entity's registered headcount and refuse to approve any supply if the client is not compliant with Saudization such that it has achieved at least a medium green compliance category.

With regard to secondment and business-to-business (B2B) services, the Ajeer portal provides as follows. Both companies must be in category low green for Saudization compliance purposes. Essentially the portal acts as an electronic approval process for individuals to be seconded from one entity to another for a period of six months. Entities permitted to use this service include the following sectors: construction, pharmacies, and consultancy services. Ajeer also permits women who are sponsored by their husbands to work within the education sector.

Ajeer for Business Services (B2B) targets the business sector and aims at documenting the contractual relationship between a service provider's client and the expatriate worker who will be working at the client's site. Such a contractual relationship can arise from a sub-contract or a direct service contract between the service provider and the client. To that end, Ajeer grants temporary work notices (TWN) that are issued by the service provider to each expatriate employee that will be working at a client's site. Whilst the client can be either an individual or an entity, the service provider must be registered with Nitaqat to perform certain activities which are currently limited to: (1) building and construction, (2) contracting of maintenance, (3) cleaning, (4) operation and sustenance, (5) consulting and business services, and (6) institutes and colleges.

In addition to TWNs, Ajeer also provides secondment notices (SNs) to expatriate employees who have been seconded to a client's site for a specific period of time. This type of notice is currently limited to expatriate pharmacists working in pharmacies (based on certain conditions) and expatriate employees of building and construction entities only. The main condition for issuing SNs is that both the service provider and the client are licensed to conduct the same business activities.

B2B enables employers to issue TWNs for contracts as well as issuing SNs for the authorized economic activities pursuant to the KSA Labour Law and regulations through the Ajeer online portal. TWNs are issued against a fee of up to SAR 20 per expatriate employee and validity of up to six months which may be renewed. SNs are issued against a fee of SAR 60 per expatriate employee and a validity of three months which may be renewed.

The liability of issuing the above notices falls on the service provider/seconding entity which must ensure the following:

(i) the relevant expatriate employee has been in the KSA for more than three months;
(ii) the expatriate employee has a valid residency visa (Iqama);
(iii) Company A's Saudi postal delivery service 'Wasel' is activated;
(iv) all of Company A's required licenses and registrations are valid;
(v) both Company A and its client must be at least in the low green Nitaqat category; and
(vi) the service contract is attested by the Chamber of Commerce and Industry (CoC) – There is no requirement of registering such contract with the MOL. The client should only ensure its validity and attestation from the CoC in case a MOLSD inspector asks to see it.

8.5. Checklist of Do's and Don'ts

(1) Ensure that there is always a written agreement with individuals clarifying their employment status, the services they are expected to provide and the hours they are expected to work.
(2) When engaging with a manpower supplier always request a copy of their trade licence to ensure that they are properly licensed to provide the services.
(3) Register for Ajeer in order to be able to provide or to receive seconded employees.

9. OBLIGATION TO BARGAIN COLLECTIVELY WITH TRADE UNIONS: EMPLOYEES' RIGHT TO STRIKE AND A COMPANY'S RIGHT TO CONTINUE BUSINESS OPERATIONS

9.1. Overview of Unions' Right to Organize

Trade unions and labour associations are unlawful in KSA with the KSA Penal Code outlawing labour strikes. However, the KSA Labour Law contains a workforce disputes procedure under which employees may collectively submit a written complaint to the Ministry of Labour which will appoint a labour committee to investigate the complaint and conciliate between the employees and the employer. Workers are also permitted to form Welfare Committees for social welfare within the workplace. KSA national employees are also permitted to form work councils.

10. WORKING CONDITIONS: HOURS OF WORK AND PAYMENT OF WAGES – BY STATUTE OR COLLECTIVE AGREEMENTS

10.1. Overview of Wages and Hours Laws

a. Working Hours

The maximum working hours (except for senior employees or managers, who are exempt from the relevant provisions) are eight hours per day or forty-eight hours per six-day week. However, the Government has for some time indicated that it plans to implement a two day weekend for the private sector which would see the working week reduced to forty hours. When this will come into force, and how it will be implemented is not yet clear. The Labour Law stipulates that an employee's total working hours (including overtime) should not exceed ten hours per day or sixty hours per week under any circumstances. Furthermore, workers should not work for more than five consecutive hours without a break of at least thirty minutes in any working day and should not remain at the workplace for more than twelve hours a day in total (of which one hour must be for rest, food and prayer).

Certain sectors are permitted to operate a nine-hour day, and some are required to operate a seven-hour day (if necessary for health and safety reasons). These sectors are determined by ministerial decree.

The MOLSD currently restricts overtime hours to a maximum of seven hundred and twenty hours per annum. However, employers and employees can agree further overtime hours provided they do so in writing.

Friday is the official day of rest with Saturday generally being the other weekend day in KSA. Working hours are reduced to six hours a day or thirty-six hours per week during Ramadan for fasting Muslim employees only. It is permitted to agree in writing with an employee that his weekly rest day will be a day other than Friday (traders within financial institutions will often agree this). If the employee is a Muslim, then he must be given time off on Friday to attend prayers.

Furthermore, in addition to the rest periods granted to all workers, a female employee is entitled to one hour break per day to nurse her child following her return to work which is calculated as part of the employee's working hours and is paid.

b. Wages

The Labour Law uses the following concepts in connection with the definition of remuneration:

(1) Basic Wages – monies given to the employee by virtue of a written or unwritten employment contract regardless of the kind of wage or its method of payment, in addition to periodic payments.
(2) Actual Wages – Basic Wages plus all other payments including commissions, productivity-linked payments, work allowances, standard of living and family allowances, bonuses, and 'in rem' privileges (defined as what the employer commits to provide the worker in the employment contract or work regulations up to a maximum of two months′ basic wage per annum, unless otherwise stipulated).

Employees may be remunerated on a monthly, weekly or daily basis.

c. Wages Protection System

In September 2013, KSA commenced the implementation of the WPS. The WPS monitors the payment of wages to both KSA and non-KSA nationals employed in the private sector, establishing a link between the employer, the local bank into which wages must be paid, and the employee. The WPS has been phased in and now applies to registered commercial entities with eighty or more employees and all private schools (regardless of the number of employees).

The recent amendments to the Labour Law introduced a requirement for employee's salary to be paid into an employee's bank account through approved banks. Remuneration may also include a cost of living allowance or other bonuses or allowances provided for in the employment contract or in the internal regulations of the company. Under the Labour Law, wages must be paid in the national currency but, in practice, are paid in any currency agreed between the parties (other than restricted currencies, for example, Israeli Sheqels).

10.2. Minimum Wage

There is no national minimum wage in KSA. However, the Labour Law does reserve to the Council of Ministers the power to impose a minimum wage upon a recommendation by the Minister of Labour. In order for a KSA national to be counted under regulations regarding the employment of nationals in the private sector, the KSA national must be paid a monthly salary of at least SAR 3,000.

10.3. Overtime

Total working hours should not exceed ten hours per day or sixty hours per week. Work in excess of the statutory working week is compensated at 100% of hourly wages plus 50% of basic wages. Overtime in a year should normally be no more than seven hundred and twenty hours.

10.4. Meal and Rest Periods

Workers should not work for more than five consecutive hours without a break of at least thirty minutes in any working day and should not remain at the workplace for more than twelve hours a day in total (of which one hour must be for rest, food and prayer).

10.5. Deductions from Wages

An employer must not deduct any amount from the employee's salary without the employee's written consent, except for the purpose of:

(1) the repayment of any loans extended by the employer, provided that such deductions do not exceed 10% of the employee's wage;
(2) social insurance or any other contributions due to the workers as provided for by law;
(3) the worker's contributions to thrift funds or loans due to such funds;

(4) instalments of any scheme undertaken by the employer involving home ownership programmes or any other privilege;
(5) fines imposed on the worker on account of violations of the Labour and/or internal policies, as well as deductions made for damages caused; or
(6) any debt collected in implementation of a judicial judgment, provided that the monthly deduction shall not exceed one-quarter of the worker's wage unless the judgment provides otherwise.

10.6. Garnishment

Attachments to earnings are possible through a court order, and deductions may be made accordingly by an employer.

10.7. Exemptions to Wage and Hours Laws

The Labour Law exempts the following categories of employees from restrictions on working time:

(1) Persons occupying high positions of authority in management and policy, if such positions grant the persons occupying them authority over workers.
(2) Preparatory or supplemental works which must be completed before or after the commencement of work.
(3) Work that is intermittent by necessity.
(4) Guards and janitors, excluding civil security guards.

10.8. Child Labour

The following provisions apply to minors:

(1) The minimum employment age is age 15; however, the Labour Law empowers the MOLSD to raise the minimum age for certain industries or categories of minors. Conversely, the MOLSD may also permit the employment of children age 13 to age 15 in light work, provided that the work is not potentially harmful to their health or growth and does not hinder or impair their schooling.
(2) Minors are not permitted to work more than six hours per day, which is reduced to four hours per day during the month of Ramadan.
(3) Minors are not permitted to remain in the workplace for more than seven hours per day and must not work for more than four consecutive hours without a period of rest of at least half an hour.

(4) Minors are not permitted to work during weekly rest days or official holidays.
(5) Minors are not permitted to work during the night unless explicitly permitted by the MOLSD.
(6) Minors may not be employed in hazardous jobs or harmful industries or in occupations or jobs that may endanger their health, safety or morals due to the nature or conditions of the same; and
(7) prior to employing a minor, an employer must obtain from him his national identification card or an official birth certificate, a report of physical fitness for the required job issued by a competent physician and duly certified by a health authority and the consent of the minor's guardian.

10.9. Record-Keeping Requirements

a. Information That Must Be Maintained

Employers are required to include the following data in the records, statements and files kept at the workplace, whether paper or electronic:

(1) statement of the workers' names: containing all the names of the establishment's workers, their respective professions, ages, nationalities, ID numbers and work permit numbers and dates for non-Saudi nationals;
(2) statement of workers' wages: containing information on the workers' wages, date of receipt thereof, any deductions from the wage and the deduction reason;
(3) penalty record: containing a statement of the worker's name, wage, amount of the applied penalty, reason and date of penalty application;
(4) attendance record: containing the time of the worker's attendance to work and leaving the work premises and any other information added by the employer;
(5) Saudi national training record: containing the training programme's title, type, duration, year, numbers and names of trained workers and their percentage to the employer's workers. Employers are required to provide a minimum of sixteen hours of training;
(6) medical examination record for the workers in the establishments whose workers are likely to suffer from occupational diseases. This record shall contain the names of examined workers, examination date and results thereof; and
(7) a work file for every worker: containing the employee's data, address, copy of the employment contract and any certificates or documents submitted thereby to the employer.

b. Records That Must Be Maintained

Employers must keep the following records:

(1) list of workers' names;
(2) list of workers' wages;
(3) recording fines imposed on workers;
(4) attendance log;
(5) workers' medical check-ups;
(6) a work file for each worker.

c. Failure to Maintain Required Records

Failure to keep these records could result in a fine of SAR 5,000.

10.10. Reductions in Compensation Caused by Economic Downturn

Any reduction in compensation must be agreed with an employee as a matter of contract, and an employer does not have the right to unilaterally vary an employee's contractual compensation.

10.11. Checklist of Do's and Don'ts

(1) Maintain clear records as required above.
(2) Maintain records in line with the Labour Law in order to demonstrate compliance.
(3) Pay employees through the WPS, or record details of employees who are not paid through WPS and reasons why.
(4) Keep records of working hours and overtime.

11. OTHER WORKINGS CONDITIONS AND BENEFITS: BY STATUTE, COLLECTIVE AGREEMENTS OR COMPANY POLICY

11.1. Health and Other Insurance

The Saudi government provides free medical care for all Saudi citizens via an extensive network of government health clinics and hospitals. The government will also pay for services which are only available in private facilities in Saudi Arabia or abroad. Foreigners working in the public sector are entitled to free medical care at government facilities, including inpatient and outpatient treatment, prescription drugs, medical devices, therapy, and dental and optical care.

Since 2006, employers in the private sector are required to provide employees and their dependants with health insurance; dependants are spouses, unmarried daughters regardless of their age and sons under the age of 25. Employers are also obliged to provide health insurance coverage under a unified insurance policy, meaning that all employees in one establishment must be provided cover under one health insurance cover (although different levels of employees can be provided with different levels of cover – e.g. more senior employees can have enhanced cover). All health insurance policies must be local policies operated and provided in the Kingdom.

11.2. Pension and Retirement Benefits

Social security provides old-age retirement, survivors, long-term disability, and worker's compensation benefits for KSA nationals. Foreign nationals are covered only by the worker's compensation programme. The HDRF provides unemployment allowance for KSA nationals who are university graduates for a period of one year from graduation, providing SAR 2,000 a month. Unemployment benefit is also payable to KSA nationals.

The most recent social security reforms came into force in September 2002, entitling all KSA employees to an old-age social security pension (previously employees in companies with fewer than ten employees were excluded from social security coverage). The scheme is applicable to all KSA nationals, including those employed abroad not covered by the local social security system. Monthly earnings, for the purpose of social security contributions, are capped at SAR 45,000.

Retirement (as well as survivors and disability) benefits are funded by employer and employee contributions of 9% each. The minimum and maximum monthly earnings for the purposes of contributions and benefits are SAR 1,500 and SAR 45,000, respectively.

Individuals with at least one hundred twenty months of paid or credited (*see* below) contributions are eligible for an old-age pension. Individuals must retire to receive the pension. Individuals who do not meet the minimum qualifying standards for an old-age pension are entitled to a lump sum settlement.

Where an employee does not have one hundred and twenty months of paid contributions but has at least sixty months of paid contributions, they may elect to pay the remaining contributions either in one lump sum or in monthly instalments and thereby still become eligible for an old-age pension. Such 'credited contributions' cannot exceed sixty months.

Both in case of normal and early retirement, the retirement pension is calculated as follows:

(1) 2.5% of the average monthly salary over the last two years multiplied by the number of years of social security contributions up to 100% of the pension calculation base.

(2) Covered average monthly earnings cannot exceed 150% of monthly earnings subject to social security contributions at the beginning of the last five-year contribution period. Special provisions apply if the insured's monthly earnings decrease during the two years prior to retirement. The minimum monthly retirement pension is SAR 1,500. The lump sum settlement is equal to 10% of the insured's average monthly earnings in the last two years for each of the first sixty months of contributions plus 12% for each additional month.

(3) If an individual receiving an old-age pension resumes covered employment, the pension will be suspended until retirement resumes. Based on the more favourable outcome for the pensioner, the benefit will be adjusted to reflect either the prior and additional periods of contributions or only the final period of contributions.

(4) Survivor pensions are payable provided the deceased individual, at the time of death, has paid at least three consecutive or six non-consecutive months of contributions to the social security system. The system does not distinguish between survivors with regard to the division of payment. Therefore there is no difference between the pension payable to a spouse (or spouses), children, or other eligible beneficiaries.

(5) Survivors' benefits are payable to spouses, dependent sons under the age of 20 (age 25 if a full-time student), dependent unmarried daughters, and in certain circumstances, siblings, parents, grandparents, and grandchildren.

(6) The survivors' pension is based on the amount of the paid (death-in-retirement) or accrued (death-in-service) retirement pension. The pension benefit is divided equally amongst eligible survivors, at a rate equal to 100% of the old-age pension paid or payable for three or more survivors, 75% for two survivors, and 50% for one survivor. The minimum monthly individual survivors' pension is SAR 300. The minimum combined pension is equal to the greater of the deceased's average monthly earnings used to calculate the pension or SAR 1,500.

(7) Survivors of workers ineligible for an old-age pension are entitled to a share of a lump sum benefit calculated on the same basis as the

old-age retirement settlement (10% of the insured's monthly earnings in the last two years for each of the first sixty months of contributions plus 12% for each additional month).

(8) Survivors' pensions for females cease in the event of marriage or remarriage. In lieu of a pension, surviving females are entitled to a marriage grant equal to eighteen times the monthly pension amount. The pension may be reinstated in the event of subsequent divorce or widowhood. If reinstatement occurs within eighteen months of receiving the marriage grant, the balance of the remaining period will be recovered from the monthly pension.

11.3. Vacation and Holiday Payments on Termination

Employees are entitled to twenty-one calendar days' paid leave after one year's service, rising to thirty calendar days after five years.

The following are public holidays in Saudi Arabia:

(a)	Saudi National Day	23 September (if this day falls on a Thursday or Friday another day either before or after the weekend will be the holiday)
(b)	Eid al-Adha	Lunar determined (minimum 4 days)
(c)	Eid al-Fitr	Lunar determined (minimum 4 days)

Under the Labour Law, employees are entitled to full pay during the two Eid holidays.

Subject to employer agreement, employees may defer annual leave entitlements to the following year. Employers may also postpone an employee's leave for up to ninety days if required by work conditions. The leave may be further postponed with the employee's written agreement. Accrued leave entitlements cannot be postponed past the end of the year following the year that the leave is due. Upon termination of employment, employees are entitled to pay in lieu of accrued but untaken annual leave.

11.4. Leaves of Absence

a. Personal Leave

Where an employee is getting married, such employee is entitled to five days paid leave.

Employees who are undertaking further education with an education institution, who have obtained the approval of the employer are entitled to paid leave for the purposes of sitting examinations for the first time. Where they are repeating an examination, they are entitled to unpaid leave for such purpose.

b. Medical or Sick Leave

There is no social security cash sickness or short-term disability programme in KSA. Employees are entitled to one hundred and twenty days of sick leave per year. During sick leave, employees receive 100% of pay for the first thirty days, 75% of pay for the next sixty days, and no pay for the last thirty days. If further leave is required because of illness, this can be deducted from vacation entitlements, if any.

Employees may not be terminated due to illness during sick leave, however. Most multinational companies provide pay replacement benefits in excess of the statutory minimum, frequently offering full pay for three months or longer.

c. Bereavement Leave

A Muslim female employee, whose husband passes away, is entitled to paid leave for the legally prescribed waiting period (iddah) of four months and ten days from the husband's date of death. Where the spouse is pregnant additional unpaid leave may be taken until the baby is delivered.

Non-Muslim female employees, whose husband passes away, are entitled to fifteen days paid leave.

Male employees are entitled to five days paid leave in the event of the death of a spouse, ascendant or descendant.

d. Family Leave

See section 11.4 f below.

e. Pregnancy Leave

Employers are required to provide medical care for female workers during pregnancy and delivery. *See* section 11.4 f below.

f. Maternity & Paternity Leave

Maternity Leave

A female worker is entitled to a minimum of ten weeks' paid maternity leave, four weeks to be taken immediately preceding the expected date of delivery and then six weeks following the birth of the child. Under the 2015 Amendments, a female employee may now take an additional one month's unpaid maternity leave if she chooses. If the baby is ill or disabled, the mother is entitled to an additional one month paid leave. The probable date of delivery will be determined by the physician of the firm or pursuant to a medical report certified by a health authority. A woman may not work during the six week period immediately following delivery under any circumstances. There is no minimum length of service for this leave to be paid.

Companies typically supplement statutory requirements by giving an extended period of maternity leave so that the approach is in line with the general approach of other multinational companies operating in the region whose practices will be in line with those in the host jurisdiction.

Paternity Leave

Male employees are entitled to paternity leave of three days for the birth of their child. It is, however, market practice in many multinationals to offer male employees an additional period of leave.

The Labour Law also contains express paid leave provisions for marriage, education, bereavement (which have now been significantly extended) and in the event of an emergency.

g. Hajj Leave

Where an employee has completed two years' continuous employment with the same employer, he is entitled to ten to fifteen days' paid leave to perform Hajj (granted once during the course of the employee's employment).

h. Injury at Work

Employers are responsible for all accidents at work and for the safety of its employees and third parties, meaning compensation for victims and health treatment for workplace injuries. Employers should post signs in Arabic and other applicable languages detailing the health and safety procedures applicable at the relevant place of work. The Ministry of Labour may impose additional requirements or practices in line with the work being undertaken at certain premises.

Where an employee suffers a work-related accident or an occupational disease, the employer is required to immediately report the accident to the MOLSD and provide the following details with respect to the injured employee:

(1) Name
(2) Profession
(3) Address
(4) Nationality
(5) A brief description of the incident and the circumstances surrounding the incident
(6) The medical measures or treatment provided.

In order to claim GOSI benefits, the reporting procedure, given below, must be undertaken following a work-related injury or illness:

(1) The injured employee or his representative must inform the employer within seven days from the date of injury, relapse or discovery of the disease, regardless of whether or not the injury precludes the employee from continuing to perform his duties, whenever his condition so permits. Where the employee fails to comply with such reporting requirement, he may forfeit his GOSI compensation entitlements. Late reporting in certain circumstances may be accepted on a case by case basis;
(2) The employer (or his representative) is also obliged to report the injury to the local GOSI office within three days from the date of notification or knowledge of the occurrence of the injury. If the report is delayed without an acceptable reason, the employer may be held liable to pay all expenses incurred.
(3) Where the injured employee suffers a relapse or complications, the employee is obliged to update the local GOSI office who will in turn update the employee's employer.

The police must also be notified. Once reported, the police investigate and compile a report which covers the following:

(1) testimony from any witnesses, the employer or representative and those injured;
(2) whether the accident was work related;
(3) whether the accident took place intentionally; and
(4) whether the accident was the result of misbehaviour on the part of the employee.

In the case of temporary disability arising from work injury, the injured party shall be entitled to financial aid equal to his full wage for sixty days, then 75% of the wage for the entire duration of his treatment. If one year elapses or it is medically determined that the injured party's chances of recovery are improbable or that he is not physically fit to work, his injury shall be deemed total disability and the contract terminated.

If an injury results in permanent total disability or the death of the injured person, the injured person or his eligible beneficiaries shall be entitled to a compensation equal to his wages for three years, with a minimum of SAR 54,000.

If the injury results in a permanent partial disability, the injured person shall be entitled to compensation equal to the percentage of the estimated disability in accordance with the approved disability percentage guide schedule multiplied by the amount of compensation for the permanent total disability.

Employers must also register all employees with GOSI and pay contributions of 2% of basic salary and housing allowance for each employee. This insurance covers workplace injury, and if an employee suffers an injury, then GOSI regulations would also be relevant with regard to compensation payable.

i. Accommodation

Employers operating in remote locations, mines, quarries and oil exploration centres are required to provide their workers with accommodation, camps, transportation and meals. Such provisions are to be determined by the MOLSD and will also apply to marine contract work in the majority of cases.

11.5. Checklist of Do's and Don'ts

(1) Have clear company policies regarding family-friendly policies.
(2) Consider operating best practice policies with regard to paternity, maternity and adoption leave; possibly awarding unpaid leave in the absence of legislative obligations providing for paid leave.
(3) Ensure that employees are familiar with notification requirements for taking leave (of whatever nature).
(4) Ensure that health and safety policies and rules are clearly displayed, together with reporting procedures for workplace accidents.

12. WORKERS' COMPENSATION

12.1. Overview

Employers must register all employees, both Saudi nationals and foreign nationals, with GOSI and contribute 2% of basic salary and housing allowance to GOSI to cover workplace accident insurance. Accordingly, where a workplace accident occurs or a workplace disease is contracted, the process set out above should be completed, and GOSI will assess compensation due and payable.

12.2. Checklist of Do's and Don'ts

(1) Ensure GOSI contributions are made in full.
(2) Have a protocol for reporting incidents to GOSI.
(3) Consider requesting employees have annual medical examinations.

13. COMPANY'S OBLIGATIONS TO PROVIDE A SAFE AND HEALTHY WORKPLACE

13.1. Overview of Safety and Environmental Laws and Regulations

An employer's obligations regarding health and safety are set out in a variety of laws and regulations. In addition to the Labour Law, health and safety obligations are imposed by the municipality, civil defence authority and other sector regulatory authorities.

13.2. Requirements

The Labour Law obliges an employer to maintain a safe workplace for its employees providing equipment and training as appropriate for its operations. Employers must set out health and safety rules applicable in the workplace and display them prominently, ensuring employees are aware of them. They must also provide first aid kits, private medical insurance and workmen's compensation for any work-related injury or disease.

13.3. Rights of Employee

Employees should be provided with

(1) drinking water;
(2) well-ventilated working environment;
(3) restrooms;
(4) equipment necessary to perform their work;
(5) training to understand the risks of their roles and how to prevent them; and
(6) summertime break if the employee works in an exposed environment meaning that the employee must not be working outside between the hours of 12.30 to 3.30 from mid-June to mid-September.

13.4. Rights of Employer

Provided the employer fulfils his duties, an employee who breaches health and safety rules can be terminated for gross misconduct. If an employee deliberately causes an accident, no compensation will be payable. Employees can also be subject to personal fines which the employer can deduct directly through payroll such as SAR 1,000 for failure to observe health and safety rules or maintaining safety equipment or if the employee misuses or disables the means prepared for protecting the workplace and the workers' health and safety.

13.5. Specific Standards

The specific requirements are set out above.

13.6. Injury or Accident at Work

See 11.4 h above.

13.7. Workplace Violence

The MOLSD's model work regulations provide for strict prohibitions on workplace harassment and bullying. It also provides for a grievance mechanism for an employee to raise a complaint to the MOLSD which will form a committee to hear the grievance and rule on any applicable compensation or remedial action.

13.8. Fines and Penalties

The following fines may be imposed by the MOLSD for breach of health and safety obligations:

(1) Failure to take measures to ensure a safe workplace – SAR 25,000 and closure of the workplace for one day.
(2) Failure to display health and safety rules prominently in the workplace SAR 5,000.
(3) Failure to provide fire evacuation plans and equipment as well as measures for fire evacuation SAR 10,000.
(4) Failure to conduct an annual comprehensive medical examination on the employees who are exposed to any of the diseases set out in the schedule of the occupational diseases of the Social Insurance Law SAR 5,000 per employee.
(5) Requiring the worker to work under the hot sun or under bad climate condition without taking the necessary measures at the conditions, times and periods determined by a decision of the Minister SAR 3,000 per employee.
(6) Failure to provide first aid kits (stocked as required) SAR 10,000.
(7) Failure to comply with health and safety regulations SAR 15,000.
(8) Failure to provide medical health insurance SAR 10,000.

If an employer is discovered to be repeating a breach, for which the employer has previously been fined, then the fine is doubled on the second violation. A breach should be rectified within one month of being discovered and the fine imposed; otherwise the fine is regarded as a second violation and is doubled. If twenty-four months pass between one violation and a second one the second is regarded as a new violation and not a repeat one. An employer may appeal a fine within 60 days of it being imposed, but the fine itself will not be suspended pending the appeal unless by a specific committee decision of the MOLSD.

Fines are payable within fifteen days of being imposed, even where a fine is appealed, it is still payable unless suspended through a specific request by the MOSLD appeal commission.

13.9. Checklist Do's and Don'ts

(1) Carry out due diligence on what laws apply.
(2) Carry out a risk assessment to determine workplace risks.
(3) Provide drinking water.
(4) Provide well-ventilated workplaces.

(5) Provide first aid kits – one per fifty employees.
(6) Comply with summer break rules.
(7) Display health and safety rules prominently.
(8) Formulate and display fire evacuation rules.

14. IMMIGRATION, SECONDMENT AND FOREIGN ASSIGNMENT

14.1. Overview Laws Controlling Immigration

Every non-GCC national working and residing in KSA must be sponsored to do so by a KSA-based employer. As such there is no recognition within the KSA Labour Law framework for secondments; as there must always be a local employer and a local employment contract; the only exception being those entering under temporary work visas. The main piece of legislation relating to foreign nationals working in KSA is residence Permit Law (the 'Iqama Law') and all amendments hitherto, Royal Decree No. 17-2/25/1337, dated 11/09/1371 H (corresponding to 29 May 1977); There are also relevant provisions in the KSA Labour Law, the Regulations and various Ministerial Resolutions issued by MOI issued from time to time.

Under the KSA immigration regulations, an individual must:

(1) only work for his sponsor; and
(2) work in the capacity or profession stated in the residence visa ('Iqama').

The KSA Labour Law makes it clear that both the MOLSD and the MOI are now responsible for inspecting premises of companies and can take punitive measures against both the individual employee and the employer for violation of the KSA Labour Law (in addition to any other entity, or person, playing a role in the violation). Furthermore, the MOLSD is currently sending out inspectors to conduct inspections periodically to ensure compliance and application of the regulations.

14.2. Recruiting, Screening and Hiring Process

See section 3.2. Employers are free to set their own recruitment process and to request candidates to undergo third-party pre-employment checks with the key being to obtain employee consent in writing. The immigration process for non-GCC nationals requires the employee to submit a certificate of good conduct, meaning a certificate showing that he is free of a criminal conviction.

14.3. THE OBLIGATION OF EMPLOYER TO ENFORCE IMMIGRATION LAWS

It is an employer's duty to comply with the immigration regulations and ensure that any non-GCC individual engaged in working for it in the Kingdom is properly sponsored by it for work and residency purposes. The costs of recruitment (recruitment agency fees and the visa application costs as well as the flight to come to the Kingdom to take up employment) must be paid by the employer.

14.4. FINES AND PENALTIES

Failure to comply with the immigration regulations attract the following potential fines:

(1) enables the non-Saudi employee to work without obtaining a work permit or renew same: SAR 20,000 per employee;
(2) enables the non-Saudi employee to practice an occupation not included in the work permit: SAR 10,000;
(3) employing individuals sponsored as accompanying dependents without obtaining a valid permit in accordance with the conditions and procedures laid down by the MOLSD: SAR 25,000;
(4) charges the employee the fees or costs which it is required to pay: SAR 10,000 per employee;
(5) employing non-Saudis in occupations reserved for Saudis: SAR 20,000 per employee;
(6) the individual can be deported and face a lifetime ban on re-entering the Kingdom; and
(7) the employer can be banned from bidding or securing Government contracts for five years.

14.5. SECONDMENT/FOREIGN ASSIGNMENT

Secondments and foreign assignments are not recognized in KSA, and there must always be a local employment contract with the KSA entity sponsoring the individual for work and residency visa purposes. The KSA Labour Law will apply in full and on completion of the secondment or assignment, the local employment contract will be terminated, with terminable severance being payable.

14.6. Checklist of Do's and Don'ts

(1) Ensure all individuals engaged by the company are properly sponsored for work and residency purposes.
(2) Ensure all recruitment costs are born by the employer.
(3) Ensure all individuals are engaged on local contracts and appropriate accruals are made.

15. RESTRICTIVE COVENANTS AND PROTECTION OF TRADE SECRETS AND CONFIDENTIAL INFORMATION

15.1. Overview

The Labour Law entitles an employer to agree in writing with the employee that he will not compete with the employer for a period of up to two years provided the restriction is reasonable in terms of scope of the work restricted, the geographical remit and the duration.

15.2. The Law of Trade Secrets

KSA has no written penal code, and its Islamic Sharia system provides for a number of criminal offences including breach of privacy and confidentiality. An employer seeking to rely on this protection must establish that it has appropriately notified employees of information regarded as confidential and which must not be disclosed. Employees should countersign confidentiality policies and non-disclosure agreements in order to evidence their understanding and agreement.

Employers should also be aware that there is no presumption that an employer owns IP created by an employee during his employment and it is not possible to sign away rights in future IP not created at the time of employee assignment. Employees should be required to assign IP created by them through regular assignments to their employer where an employer wishes to protect its position.

15.3. Restrictive Covenants and Non-compete Agreements

Whilst clauses such as non-compete, non-solicitation and non-dealing are commonplace and permitted by law; they are very difficult to enforce against employees due to the reluctance of the Sharia Courts and the Labour Commissions to grant injunctive relief in the employment context. Often where an employer seeks to enforce such restrictions, the Sharia Courts and the Labour Commission will insist that the employer proves damage or harm suffered and will only award damages on this basis. The use of liquidated damages in agreements to enhance the enforceability of such restrictions is, therefore, commonplace.

For non-Saudi and non-GCC national employees, employers may apply to the MOLSD for a three-year ban on the employee being able to take up another job with another employer in the Kingdom following the termination of the employee's employment. Such applications are rare, given that the resolution permitting such action dates to the 1970s and very few employers are aware of its provisions.

15.4. Checklist of Do's and Don'ts

(1) Ensure that only senior employees have post-termination restrictions in their employment contracts.
(2) Ensure that post-termination restrictions are correctly drafted and countersigned by employees.
(3) Notify employees in writing of what the company regards as confidentiality information and obtain their countersignatures to notifications.
(4) Password protect confidential documents and mark them as confidential.
(5) Ensure that employees are notified that their use of communications systems (emails, internal use and other communications) will be monitored.

16. PROTECTION OF WHISTLEBLOWING CLAIMS

16.1. Overview

There is no special protection provided to whistleblowers and no definition of whistleblowing. In fact, anonymous evidence or testimonies carry very little weight and are likely to be disregarded. However, as a matter of best practice and against a wider global backdrop of increasing regulation and reporting requirements many corporations do have locally applicable whistleblowing policies and hotlines to encourage a culture of compliance and good governance. Within KSA, there is also a growing Government initiative to tackle corruption, and the Anti-corruption Commission was formed to promote a culture of good governance. An internal circular addressed to Ministries and Government Departments was also issued on 2

May 2018 prohibiting government departments falling under the jurisdiction of the National Anti-corruption Commission from taking disciplinary action or prejudicing an employee in any way as a result of the employee reporting financial or administrative corruption practices within their relevant government department. Many regulatory authorities also have codes of conduct applicable to individuals engaging in certain sectors or activities, for example, pharmacists and medical professionals from the Ministry of Health, and financial services from the Saudi Arabian Monetary Authority.

16.2. Checklist of Do's and Don'ts

(1) Have a written staff policy on business ethics and codes of conduct.
(2) Ensure employees countersign a written confirmation that they have reviewed it and agree to it.
(3) Ensure employee training is delivered on a regular basis and documented through attendance records.
(4) When carrying out an investigation, consideration should be given on whether to ensure anonymity for any individuals involved.

17. PROHIBITION OF DISCRIMINATION IN THE WORKPLACE

17.1. Overview of Anti-discrimination Laws

Whilst Islamic Sharia promotes a strong principle of equality, the Labour Law does not contain any anti-discrimination provisions applicable within the employment context. The Labour Law does promote equal pay for men and women performing the same role and also obliges an employer to promote the employment of disabled Saudi employees.

17.2. Sex Discrimination/Sexual Harassment

Until recently the KSA did not have a standalone anti-harassment law, harassment was considered unlawful under general Islamic Sharia principles. However, Decision No. 488 dated 14/9/1439 H, which was recently published in the Legal Gazette on 24 Ramadan 1439 H, equivalent to 8 June 2018 ('Anti-Harassment Law') strengthens this position as it sets out clear penalties for violation of its provisions which are designed to ensure individual autonomy and security.

The new law is far-reaching in its application, as it is not restricted to women and applies to any individual regardless of gender. It aims to protect individuals from words, acts, implicit behaviour or innuendo of a sexual nature by one individual against another targeting that individual's body, modesty or personal life by any means including modern technology and communications. The law aims to protect an individual's dignity, privacy and personal freedom in accordance with Islamic Sharia rules and regulations and imposes a duty on any individuals suffering or witnessing alleged harassment to report the allegations. Public authorities are also able to raise complaints in the public interest and all organizations whether government or non-governmental and in particular within an employment context are under an obligation to take steps to prevent harassment occurring.

Employers are under an express obligation to:

(1) put in place an internal complaints mechanism and procedure;
(2) put in place procedures to investigate complaints validity as well as ensure their confidentiality;
(3) take remedial action with regard to any breaches of these policies and the obligations under this law on employers; and
(4) not seek to prevent or replace (e.g. through trying to replace the criminal process under the law with an internal process) a victim's right to raise a complaint to the authorities regarding any harassment.

Failure to comply with the new law can result in quite severe penalties and punishment being imposed. In addition to any other potential penalty or punishment under general Islamic Sharia principles (which could include public lashing) or any other harsher punishment under other laws, penalties for breach of the law are:

(1) two-year prison sentence and/or a fine of SAR 100,000;
(2) five-year prison sentence and/or a fine of SAR 300,000 if the victim of the harassment is a child, a person of special needs, if the perpetrator was in a position of power or influence over the victim, if the harassment occurs at a place of work, education or child care, if the victim and the perpetrator are of the same sex, if the victim was sleeping or unconscious, or if the harassment occurs at a time of crisis, accident, or disaster.

17.3. Handicap and Disability Discrimination

Under Article 28 of the Labour Law, an employer is under a duty to promote the employment of Saudi disabled employees and to facilitate their employment by making adjustments to the workplace.

The Implementing Regulations elaborate on this duty clarifying that in order to have the protection of the relevant provisions, the individual must be registered with the GOSI as disabled and have a GOSI certificate. A GOSI certificate is obtained through obtaining a medical report issued by the Ministry of Health or hospitals in other government sectors. The individual also requires an ID card from the Ministry of Social Affairs and from the Ministry of Labour identifying the type and degree of his disability.

Disabilities covered by the relevant provisions are vision disability, hearing impairment, mental disability, physical disability, motion disability, learning difficulties, speech and language disorders, behavioural disorders, emotional disorders, autism or any other disability requiring any form of facilitating arrangements and services.

The Labour Law and the Implementing Regulations permit an employer to apply the same standards of competency and skill requirements of disabled employees as of other employees. The key is that they are entitled to assistance in order to meet those requirements by way of engineering modifications, adaptations of work conditions and the work environment. Annex 2 of the Implementing Regulations specify a number of adjustments which should be made with reference to specific disabilities. For example, these adjustments include:

(1) providing adequate washroom facilities, adjusted heights for shelves and facilities;
(2) computer software converting speech to text, adjustable keyboards, computers which can be controlled by feet, lips or mouth, screen readers;
(3) provision of adjusted cars;
(4) sign language interpreter or training another member of staff in sign language; and
(5) suitable ergonomic chairs.

The Implementing Regulations also state that disabled employees should not suffer any discrimination with regard to wages due to their disability and should not be excluded from vocational training, promotion, or continued employment due to their disability. An employer is also under a duty to maintain records setting out the number of employees with disabilities, the jobs they occupy, wages and type of adjustments which have been made (whether physical adjustments or additional supportive services being provided). This information may be requested by labour inspectors.

Given these significant provisions in the Labour Law and the Implementing Regulations, disabled employees are empowered to seek employment and insist on equal treatment with other employees as well as request adjustments from their employer. If an employer failed or refused to make adequate provisions, then an individual could complain to the Ministry of Labour and the Labour Commission for a breach of the law. Whilst there is strictly speaking no free-standing claim of discrimination to be raised, an employee is able to complain about specific breaches of these obligations.

17.4. Pregnancy Discrimination

Serving notice whilst an employee is on leave is not permissible under the Labour Law. However, there are no specific provisions in the Labour Law providing for the right to return to work following maternity leave to the same or a similar role or prohibiting termination due to the employee being pregnant or having taken maternity leave. It is, however, likely that any such termination would be held to be unfair.

17.5. Sexual Orientation Discrimination

Sexual acts between members of the same sex are unlawful.

17.6. Retaliation

There are no special provisions protecting individuals from retaliatory acts by employers. However, general protection from unjustified termination is provided in the Labour Law.

17.7. Constructive Discharge

Article 81 of the Labour Law sets out a list of circumstances or reasons under which an employee can resign and regard himself as being dismissed by his employer. These reasons are:

(1) failure to fulfil essential contractual obligations;
(2) fraud;
(3) assigning work differently to work agreed without consent;
(4) commit violent assaults;
(5) cruelty, injustice or insulting;
(6) failure to remove hazard threatening safety of workplace;
(7) violation of terms of contract.

17.8. Checklist of Do's and Don'ts

(1) With respect to the newly published Anti-harassment Law, as well as taking the steps specified by the new law, employers should also do the following:
  - train staff on their complaints process and the provisions of the new law, placing it within the context of workplace culture and codes of conduct;
  - remind staff of the provisions of the Model Work Regulations which require all employees to behave appropriately in the workplace;
  - consider whether other workplace policies need to be revised or highlighted for example dress codes, social media policies or confidentiality procedures; and
  - consider whistleblowing policies and procedures given the reporting duties under the new law as well as within the context of an increasing culture of compliance.

(2) Consider adopting an equal opportunities policy.
(3) Consider whether any employees on secondment or assignment are covered by discrimination legislation in their home country.
(4) Assess the impact of any recruitment or other policies on employees and their potential membership of protected classes.

18. SMOKING IN THE WORKPLACE

18.1. Overview

Smoking in the workplace is prohibited.

18.2. Checklist of Do's and Don'ts

(1) Notify all employees of the prohibition on smoking.
(2) Monitor employees' smoking breaks in order to minimize them.

19. USE OF DRUGS AND ALCOHOL IN THE WORKPLACE

19.1. Overview

Drugs and Alcohol are prohibited in Saudi Arabia. Employers can carry out random drug and alcohol testing of employees using the MOLSD's accredited system and registered government-designated clinics. This service is particularly common in the oil and gas industry.

19.2. Checklist of Do's and Don'ts

(1) Notify all employees of a zero tolerance to drugs and alcohol.
(2) Ensure the disciplinary policy makes it clear that the use of alcohol or drugs will be a disciplinary offence possibly resulting in termination.

20. AIDS, HIV, SARS, BLOODBORNE PATHOGENS

20.1. Overview

Under the immigration procedures, non-Saudi national employees must undergo a medical check. When an expatriate is recruited, he or she must obtain a medical examination certificate in his or her home country including a negative test for contagious diseases (particularly HIV) and up-to-date vaccinations (including meningococcal, hepatitis A and B and, depending on the home country, typhoid).

20.2. Checklist of Do's and Don'ts

Ensure employees are aware of the requirement for a medical examination as part of the sponsorship application and renewal process.

21. DRESS AND GROOMING REQUIREMENTS

21.1. Overview

Employees are required to comply with the requirements of Islamic Sharia. The Labour Law permits employers to have in place a requirement for employees to wear a uniform. It also provides that women must cover themselves in loose, non-transparent clothing, which in practice requires shoulders, chest and legs to be covered. In public places, it is customary for women, foreign and local to wear an abaya and for Saudi women to wear a headscarf.

In the workplace, employers are required to operate segregated workplaces, with separate working sections for men and women, including a separate entrance for women. Employers are also required to provide seating areas for women for the purpose of rest breaks. Failure to provide these can result in substantial fines being imposed.

21.2. Checklist of Do's and Don'ts

(1) Maintain a company dress policy and ensure employees are familiar with it.
(2) Remind employees regularly of the policy.
(3) Ensure compliance with segregation requirements and ensure employees understand what is expected of them in this regard.

22. PRIVACY, TECHNOLOGY AND TRANSFER OF PERSONAL DATA

22.1. Privacy Rights of Employees

There is no general data protection law applicable in KSA, but Islamic Sharia recognizes the right to privacy. Employers wishing to monitor communications or prevent personal use of the IT and communications system by employees should have written IT policies and reserve the right to monitor employees in employment contracts. KSA also has a cybercrime law prohibiting the misuse of the internet and electronic communications.

22.2. Checklist of Do's and Don'ts

(1) Have a written policy setting out permitted use of the internet and IT system.
(2) Reserve the right to monitor employee communications in employment contracts.
(3) Provide for pop up messages when employees access the internet to remind them that use of the internet is monitored.

23. WORKPLACE INVESTIGATIONS FOR COMPLAINTS OF DISCRIMINATION, HARASSMENT, FRAUD, THEFT AND WHISTLEBLOWING

23.1. Overview

Employers should be aware that the recognition and principle of legal privilege are narrow in scope. All documents created as part of an internal investigation should be labelled private and confidential. The involvement of an external legal counsel will not render the documents produced or the investigation legally privileged. Moreover, if a police report is made for suspected criminal behaviour, the police will often require a report to be compiled of the evidence and an assessment of the evidence and alleged actions to be produced by an expert. The expert should usually be one who is listed as one recognized or registered by the UAE Courts to act as an expert in civil and criminal matters.

23.2. Checklist of Do's and Don'ts

(1) Decide who will be part of the investigatory team early on when the decision is made to investigate.
(2) Keep the investigatory team small and have one contact to liaise with external counsel.
(3) Mark all documents as private and confidential and password protect them and encrypt them where possible.
(4) Manage the message internally regarding the employee(s) who are the subject of the investigation carefully to avoid any suggestion or allegation of defamation, which is a criminal offence.
(5) Consider whether an expert needs to be instructed to produce a report to be used for a police complaint or as part of a civil claim.

24. AFFIRMATIVE ACTION/NON-DISCRIMINATION REQUIREMENTS

24.1. Overview

There are extensive Saudization requirements as discussed in section 3. There are limited discrimination prohibitions within an employment context.

24.2. Checklist of Do's and Don'ts

(1) Ensure that Saudization quotas are understood and met.
(2) Ensure that the business has a plan for Saudization in terms of graduate recruitment, internships and student placements, as well as long-term succession planning.
(3) Ensure that requirements with regard to training are understood and implemented.
(4) Ensure that disabled applicants are encouraged to apply and are recruited – carry out due diligence or audit of recruitment procedures and sources for recruitment of candidates.

25. RESOLUTION OF LABOUR, DISCRIMINATION AND EMPLOYMENT DISPUTES: LITIGATION, ARBITRATION, MEDIATION AND CONCILIATION

25.1. Overview

The main court is the Sharia'a Court, which operates within the Ministry of Justice and deals with family, real estate and criminal matters. Appeals are made to the Sharia'a Court of Appeals, and subsequently to the Custodian of the Two Holy Mosques.

Disputes regarding commercial and labour matters are addressed by the MOLSD, with the Commission for the Settlement of Labour Disputes dealing with labour disputes and criminal violations of the Labour Law. It has been announced that labour disputes will in the future be transferred to the remit of the Ministry of Justice and fall within the general Sharia Courts.

Cases involving claims under the Labour Law or arising out of employment contracts will be accepted by the relevant labour office only within twelve months of termination. Further, any complaint regarding a breach of the Labour Law, a regulation or a decision must be brought within twelve months of the violation occurring. However, in practice, employees can bring claims within twelve months of termination for violations that occur during the course of employment.

25.2. Internal Dispute Resolution Process

Employee complaints or disputes should be brought to one of the thirty-seven labour offices which mediate labour disputes. Before commencing litigation, the parties should attempt to resolve disputes internally. Even once a claim has been made, the relevant labour office will propose a settlement to the parties, which they are free to accept or reject.

25.3. Mediation and Conciliation

Before commencing litigation, the parties should seek to resolve disputes internally and, even following a claim being made, a settlement will be proposed to the parties by the relevant labour office committee which they are open to accept or reject. To the extent a settlement cannot be achieved in this way, the claim will be heard by one of the labour dispute settlement committees.

25.4. Arbitration

Arbitration is rarely used in employment disputes due to the high cost and expenses that may be incurred by the parties; however, the Labour Law does not preclude arbitration as an option for resolving employment disputes.

25.5. Litigation

Where a settlement cannot be achieved, the claim will be heard by one of the labour dispute settlement committees. Decisions of the initial committee may be appealed within thirty days of receiving the judgment. If the decision is not appealed within the specified period, it shall be deemed final and enforceable.

The powers of appeal are with the High Commission which presides over the labour dispute settlement committees. The High Commission has the power to re-visit part or all of the specific case and, if necessary, summon any person for interrogation or assign one of its members to conduct such interrogation. It may also require submission of documents and evidence and take any other measures it may deem fit. The Commission also has the right of access to any premises of the company for the purpose of conducting investigations and reviewing all books, records and documents it deems necessary.

25.6. Fines, Penalties and Damages

The Labour Law provides a dispute resolution framework and sets out fines and punishment regime for specific offences under the Labour Law.

The employer and any of its sites or premises at any time may be subject to inspection by officials from the MOLSD, who will monitor compliance with the provisions of the Labour Law and other laws and regulations. Breaches of the Labour Law or other regulations could lead to fines, a freeze on the company's ability to obtain work permits for new employees, and ultimately even the cancellation of its trade licence.

25.7. Checklist of Do's and Don'ts

All relevant papers will need to be submitted in Arabic and translated by an official translator in order to be submitted for use in a labour dispute settlement committee.

26. EMPLOYER RECORD-KEEPING, DATA PROTECTION, AND EMPLOYEE ACCESS TO PERSONNEL FILES AND RECORDS

26.1. Overview

There is no overarching data protection law in the Kingdom. There are cybercrimes law and general principles within Islamic Sharia protecting confidentiality. Under the Labour Law, an employer must maintain various personnel files, and these can be held electronically or in hard copy. Employees do not have an express right to access their information, but they potentially could raise a claim for damages if their information was misused on the basis of having suffered direct harm.

26.2. Personnel Files

Employers are obliged to maintain various personnel records as set out in section 10.9.

26.3. Confidentiality Rules

There is no general data protection law, but there is a duty to maintain the confidentiality of personal information.

26.4. Employee Access

An individual has no express or regulated right to request access to the information an employer holds on him or her.

27. REQUIRED NOTICES AND POSTINGS

27.1. Overview

An employer has to display publicly and prominently certain rules applicable within the workplace, and these include those on health and safety and working hours.

27.2. Checklist of Do's and Don'ts

(1) Working hours should be displayed in the workplace depending on the sector or type of environment, e.g. manufacturing and construction.
(2) Health and safety rules should be displayed in all workplaces.
(3) Employees should be notified if their communications or use of the IT system is monitored.